SCANDINAVIAN
CROSS STITCH DESIGNS

Also by Jana Hauschild Lindberg
and published by Cassell:

Making Gifts in Counted Cross Stitch (1990)
Flowers in Cross Stitch (1992)
Cross Stitch Animals (1994)

SCANDINAVIAN
CROSS STITCH DESIGNS

JANA HAUSCHILD LINDBERG

CASSELL

A CASSELL BOOK

First published in the UK 1996
by Cassell
Wellington House
125 Strand
LONDON
WC2R 0BB

Distributed in the United States
by Sterling Publishing Co., Inc.
387 Park Avenue South, New York,
NY 10016-8810

Distributed in Australia
by Capricorn Link (Australia) Pty Ltd
2/13 Carrington Road, Castle Hill NSW 2154

A British Library Cataloguing in Publication
Data block for this book may be obtained from
the British Library

ISBN 0-304-34389-7
Typeset by Keystroke, Jacaranda Lodge,
Wolverhampton
Printed and bound in Spain

CONTENTS

INTRODUCTION

Scandinavia is a fairly homogeneous area. For centuries the three countries have been under each other's influence through successive unions – Denmark-Norway, Norway-Sweden, even all three together – and although these have always ended in battle, the cultural, traditional and artistic links between the three peoples remain strong to this day.

Despite these close ties, each country has succeeded in retaining its own individual character, and this is reflected in the wonderfully rich variety of artistic treasures to be found in museums and exhibitions throughout Scandinavia. Many of the cross stitch embroidery designs in this book have been inspired by items discovered in these collections, ranging from fifth-century woven textiles, through traditional folk art patterns and eighteenth-century porcelain designs, to original paper cuts made by the famous Danish fairy-story teller, Hans Christian Andersen. For other designs I have drawn upon traditional Scandinavian symbols and motifs that have been handed down from generation to generation, and upon the beautiful natural environment and wildlife of the region.

The Vikings were ancestors to all three Scandinavian populations. A people without borders, they left their mark as far as the Urals in the east, the Mediterranean in the south, and England in the west, and relics from their time have proved an exciting source for the designs that make up the first collection in this book. The characteristic bold, yet often complex, symbolic patterning of these artefacts, frequently including wave-like fragments that echo the ocean swell so familiar to a seafaring people, stand in strong contrast to the later designs in the rest of the book.

The three collections that follow cover designs from Norway, Sweden and Denmark, each commencing with a detailed and accurate depiction of a traditional folk costume from that country. The individual character and artistic life of each country begins to emerge through the varied collections, although the strong links between the three cultures are also very much in evidence. Here are the snowflakes, stars, reindeer and Christmas trees one would expect in a Scandinavian collection, but also many more unexpected delights drawn from less well-known sources, which together make up a fascinating collection and diverse range of designs that includes something for everyone.

Finally, I have gathered together a collection of items embellished with embroideries based on traditional Christmas themes. This draws together the threads of the three Scandinavian cultures in celebration of a festival which is of great importance to them all, and the range of designs provides just a taste of the richness and diversity which unites the three countries at this time of year.

By following the detailed charts, and the accompanying project ideas and instructions which explain how to make up your finished embroideries into a huge range of items, both large and small, you will be able to recreate some of the most beautiful designs from this area of the world – and add a touch of simple Scandinavain charm to your home.

COUNTED CROSS STITCH TECHNIQUES AND PROJECTS

Counted cross stitch is one of the simplest forms of embroidery.
It consists of a series of cross stitches embroidered on an evenweave fabric over the intersection of the horizontal and vertical threads. The stitches are worked following a chart. Each cross stitch is indicated by a symbol; the different symbols represent different colours (fig. 1). You can work the design as directed in the colour key, or make up your own original colour scheme.

FISH

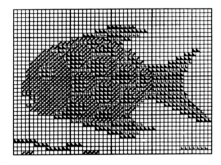

■	797	dark blue
☑	807	dark turquoise
L	598	light turquoise

The size of a cross stitch design is determined by the type of fabric upon which it is embroidered. Although finished sizes are given for the designs in this book, it is easy to calculate a different finished size by using the following formula:

**Finished size = Number of stitches
Thread count of fabric**

For example, let's say you have selected a design that is 42 stitches wide and 98 stitches long and you

would like to work on a cloth that has 5½ threads per cm (13½ threads per in). The finished width of your design can be determined by dividing the number of stitches (42) by the number of threads (5½/13½), which gives you a design that is 7.5 cm (3 in) wide. For the length, divide the number of stitches (98) by the thread count (5½/13½) to find out that the design will be 17.5 cm (7 in) long. If you feel this size is too large, try switching to a linen cloth which has 10 threads per cm (25 threads per in). The size in that case would be approximately 4 cm (1¼ in) wide by 10 cm (4 in) long. Use this formula to decide quickly which thread count of fabric is best for you to use.

MATERIALS
FABRIC
You can use any evenweave fabric made from cotton, linen, wool or synthetic blends. Cotton and linen fabrics are the most widely used. Counted-thread fabrics specially woven for cross stitch, such as Aida or Hardanger, are available in many needlecraft shops, although these are limited in colour range. Aida fabric is cotton and can be bought in three sizes: 4½, 5½ and 7 stitches per cm (11, 13½ or 18 stitches per in). Hardanger cloth is available in linen or cotton. If you would like to embroider on an unusual-coloured fabric, try using linen which is available in most fabric shops. When using linen, one has to take into account the inevitable slubs and inconsistencies that occur in the weave; this is why it is best to work counted cross stitch over two or more threads on linen fabric (see fig. 7). Thirty-count linen will give much the same effect as working on 14-count Aida cloth.

The fabrics used for the designs given in this book include linen and Aida. Linen measures are in threads. Aida measures are in stitches. Counted cross stitch designs in which the background is stitched may also be worked on needlepoint canvas. In this case, tapestry or crewel wools may be used instead of embroidery floss and other fine threads to create hardwearing cushions, footstool covers and other soft furnishing items. Please note the following:

10 threads per cm	=	25 per in
8 threads per cm	=	20 per in
6 threads per cm	=	15 per in
5½ stitches per cm	=	13½ per in
4½ stitches per cm	=	11 per in

THREADS AND YARNS
Six-strand cotton embroidery floss is ideal for counted cross stitch because the floss can be separated into the exact number of strands that provide the correct amount of coverage. Use thread or yarn that is the same thickness as the threads of the fabric you are embroidering. For flatter designs, separate the strands of floss and work with two strands in your needle. If you wish to create a more textured effect, use more strands. You can also use silk or metallic threads, Danish mohair, pearl cotton, even crewel wool, depending on the thread count of your fabric. To add some sparkle to a design, mix one strand of metallic thread with two strands of embroidery floss. Throughout this book I have referred to DMC six-strand embroidery floss. A conversion chart at the end of this chapter shows at a glance where you can make substitutions with flosses manufactured by two other companies: Royal Mouliné, or Coats/Bates Anchor.

EQUIPMENT

NEEDLES

Use a small blunt tapestry needle, size number 24 or 26, to avoid splitting the fabric threads.

HOOP

Work with a small round embroidery hoop which consists of an inner ring and an adjustable outer ring that tightens by turning a screw.

SCISSORS

You must have a pair of small sharp embroidery scissors for cutting threads and a pair of sharp fabric shears for cutting out the fabric.

TECHNIQUE

Depending upon the gift project that you would like to make (see instructions at the end of this chapter), cut your fabric to the desired size plus about 2.5 cm (1 in) around each of the edges. Overcast the edges of the fabric to prevent unravelling by hemming, zigzagging on the sewing machine or whipstitching. Find the centre of the fabric by folding it in half crosswise and lengthwise; mark the centre point with a small stitch. Then find the centre of your design (usually indicated on the charts by arrows). Do not begin your design at the centre; instead, count the number of squares on the chart from the centre point to the top, then count the same number of squares to the top of your fabric and work your first stitch there. Work the design in horizontal rows of colour from left to right. Place the fabric in the embroidery hoop so that it is taut. Adjust the tensions as you work so that the fabric is always firmly held.

Begin stitching by leaving a length of waste thread on the back of the work, securing it with your first few stitches. Fig. 2 shows how that waste thread is secured on the wrong side of the work. Insert your needle into the holes of the fabric, working one slanted stitch over the intersection of two threads from lower right to upper left as shown in fig. 3.

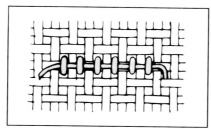

(Fig. 2)

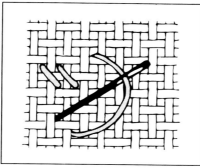

(Fig. 3)

Continue working the required number of slanting stitches across the row, following the symbols on the chart. Then work back across the row, making slanting stitches from lower left to upper right to finish each cross stitch as shown in fig. 4. (In Denmark and America, stitches are worked from lower left to upper right, then crossed from lower right to upper left. It makes no difference which way you stitch, as long as all the stitches are crossed in the same direction.)

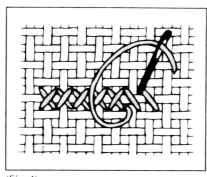

(Fig 4)

When you are working a vertical row of stitches, cross each stitch in turn as shown in fig. 5. To end a line of stitching, finish your last stitch and keep the needle and thread on the wrong side of the work. Wiggle the point of the needle beneath a few threads on the wrong side and pull the thread through as shown in fig. 6; clip off the excess thread so that the ends will not show through on the right side of the work.

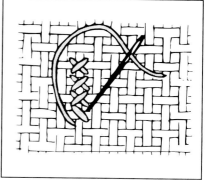

(Fig. 5)

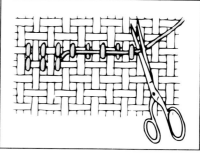

(Fig. 6)

If you are working on linen, or if you wish to make larger stitches, work over two sets of threads in each direction as shown in fig. 7. Your first few stitches may be difficult, but once you have established a row of stitches, you'll have no trouble counting two threads instead of one.

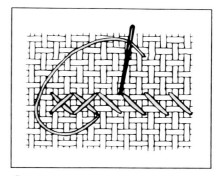

(Fig. 7)

BACKSTITCH

Backstitch is very commonly used in conjunction with counted cross stitch to outline, delineate features or emphasize a portion of the design. Work the backstitches from one hole to the next in a horizontal, vertical or diagonal direction; see fig. 8.

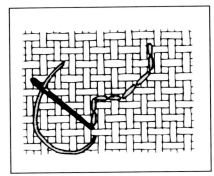

(Fig. 8)

WORKING WITH WASTE CANVAS

Counted cross stitch can be worked on non-evenweave fabrics by using a non-interlock waste canvas. Select a canvas with a stitch count of the desired size. Cut the canvas slightly larger than the finished size of your design. Baste the canvas to your chosen fabric in the area you wish to embroider. Using a crewel or chenille needle, work the design over the canvas. As you work, pass the needle straight up and down through the fabric and canvas; take great care not to catch the canvas threads in your embroidery. When the embroidery is finished, remove the basting and dampen the canvas thoroughly using a warm wet towel. Gently pull out the canvas threads one by one. Iron the finished embroidery.

SMALL QUICK PROJECTS

Instructions for making all of the projects in this book are given here unless listed under specific projects. In addition, all of the projects are adaptable and each design can be used to make any of the following items.

BOOKMARK

Cut a piece of evenweave fabric about 10 × 30 cm (4 × 11¼ in). Overcast the raw edges. Embroider a small motif or border design on the fabric, then iron the finished embroidery gently. Trim away the overcast edges. Fold the long edges to the wrong side, overlap slightly and stitch neatly in place. Carefully draw threads away from the top and bottom edges, to make fringes about 1.5 cm (½ in) deep at each end.

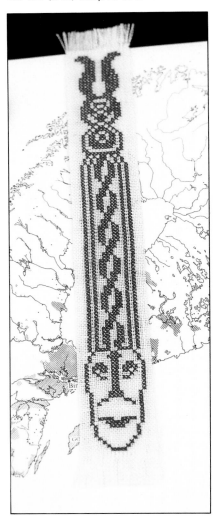

GIFT TAG, PLACECARD OR NAME LABEL

Cut evenweave fabric 2.5 cm (1 in) larger than the desired finished size. Overcast the raw edges. Embroider a small motif on the fabric; gently iron the finished embroidery. Cut away excess fabric, leaving about 1.5 cm (½ in) all around the edge of the design. Carefully draw away threads from the cut edges, creating a 6 mm (¼ in) fringe. Glue the wrong side of the design to a piece of card.

PINCUSHION OR SACHET

Cut evenweave fabric about 2.5 cm (1 in) larger than the desired finished size (or more, depending upon the size of the design). Overcast the raw edges. Embroider a small motif on the fabric; gently iron the finished embroidery. Cut away excess fabric to the desired size. Cut a matching piece of fabric for the back; stitch together with right sides facing and raw edges even, making a 6 mm (¼ in) seam and leaving an opening for turning. Turn to the right side and stuff with kapok, fibrefill or potpourri until plump. Fold in the raw edges at the opening and slipstitch the opening closed.

MATCHBOX COVER

Embroider a small motif on a piece of evenweave fabric; gently iron the finished embroidery. Cut away excess fabric to the exact size of the matchbox you wish to decorate. Glue the wrong side of the design to the top of the matchbox, making sure the raw edges are securely glued so that they do not unravel.

POCKET

Using a commercial pocket pattern, cut one pocket from evenweave fabric, adding the appropriate seam allowances. Embroider a small motif in the centre of the fabric; gently iron the finished embroidery. Cut a matching piece of fabric for the lining; stitch together with right sides facing, leaving an opening for turning. Turn to the right side, fold in the raw edges at the opening, and

slipstitch the opening closed. Iron carefully. Topstitch the edges of the pocket if desired, then sew to the front of a blouse or skirt with small slipstitches.

TIE OR COLLAR

Read the earlier instructions for working with waste canvas. Select a small design. Centre the waste canvas on a tie or collar and baste into place. Work the design over the canvas, then remove the canvas threads as directed. Iron the finished embroidery gently.

HANDKERCHIEF

Read the earlier instructions for working with waste canvas. Select a small design. Position the waste canvas in the corner of a handkerchief and baste in place. Work the design over the canvas, then remove

the canvas threads as directed. Iron the finished embroidery gently.

T-SHIRT

Read the earlier instructions for working with waste canvas. Select a medium to large design. Centre the waste canvas on the front of a T-shirt and baste in place. Work the design over the canvas, then remove the canvas threads as directed. Iron the finished embroidery gently.

BABY'S BIB

Use a piece of evenweave fabric, adding 6 mm (¼ in) all round. Overcast the raw edges. Find the centre of the bib at the neckline; begin working a small design about 2.5 cm (1 in) below the raw neck edge or in the exact centre of the bib front. Gently iron the finished embroidery. Trim away the overcast

edge. Finish the raw edges of the bib with bias binding, leaving excess binding at the back for tying.

CHRISTMAS ORNAMENTS

Cut evenweave fabric about 2.5 cm (1 in) larger than the desired finished size. Overcast the raw edges. Embroider a small motif on the fabric; gently iron the finished embroidery. Cut away excess fabric to the desired size; for a special effect, cut around the shape of the design, leaving a 6 mm (¼ in) seam allowance all around. Cut a matching piece of fabric for the back; stitch together with right sides facing and raw edges even, making a 6 mm (¼ in) seam and leaving an opening for turning. Clip any curved edges. Turn to the right side and stuff with kapok or polyester fibrefill until plump. Fold in the raw edges at the opening and slipstitch the opening closed.

UNFRAMED PICTURE

Cut a piece of evenweave fabric 2.5 cm (1 in) larger all around the desired finished size of your picture. Overcast the raw edges. Find the exact centre of the fabric and the design, and count up to the top of the design and fabric. Begin embroidering downward until the design is finished. Cut a piece of cardboard to the same size as the finished picture. Iron the embroidery carefully, wrap it around the cardboard and secure with glue.

DECORATING THE HOME

WALLHANGING

Calculate the finished size of your design using the formula on page 8; cut evenweave fabric 5 cm (2 in) larger all round than the calculated size. Overcast the raw edges. Find the exact centre of the fabric and the design and count up to the top of the design and fabric. Begin embroidering downward until the design is finished. Carefully iron the finished embroidery. Measure 3.5 cm (1½ in) from the outer edge of the embroidery at the sides and bottom and trim away the excess fabric. Trim away only the overcast edges at the top. Fold the fabric at the side and bottom edges 6 mm (¼ in) to the wrong side, then fold the fabric again 1 cm (½ in) to the wrong side. Baste, then sew the hem in place with small slipstitches. For the casing at the top edge, press the raw edge 6 mm (¼ in) to the wrong side, then fold down 2 cm (¾ in); stitch in place with small slipstitches. Iron gently. Insert a brass or wooden rod through the casing.

TABLE RUNNER

Cut a piece of evenweave fabric 2.5 cm (1 in) larger all around than the desired finished size of your table runner. Overcast the raw edges. Decide where you wish to place the design. Embroider your chosen design, adding a border all around the table runner if desired. Carefully iron the finished embroidery. Cut away excess fabric, leaving 2 cm (¾ in) for hemming. Fold the fabric 6 mm (¼ in) to the wrong side, then fold the fabric again, this time 1 cm (½ in) to the wrong side. Baste, then sew the hem in place with small slipstitches. Iron gently.

CUSHION

Calculate the finished size of your design using the formula on page 8; cut evenweave fabric 2.5 cm (1 in) larger than the calculated size all around. Overcast the raw edges. Work the design in the centre of the fabric. Carefully iron the finished embroidery. Trim away the excess fabric leaving a 1 cm (½ in) seam allowance all around. Cut a matching piece of fabric for the back. With right sides facing, stitch the back to the front, making a 6 mm (¼ in) seam and leaving an opening for turning. Turn to the right side and stuff with kapok or polyester fibrefill until plump. Fold in the raw edges at the opening and slipstitch the opening closed; alternatively fit a zipper.

BATH TOWEL EDGING

Cut evenweave fabric slightly longer than your towel and wide enough for the design plus 1 cm (½ in). Overcast the raw edges. Embroider a border design along the centre of the fabric. Gently iron the finished embroidery. Trim off the overcast edges. Fold the raw edges of the embroidery 6 mm (¼ in) to the wrong side and baste to your towel; slipstitch securely along each edge.

CURTAIN TIEBACKS OR LAMPSHADE TRIM

Cut evenweave fabric slightly longer than required and wide enough for the design plus 1 cm (½ in). Overcast the raw edges. Embroider a border design along the centre of the fabric. Gently iron the finished embroidery. Cut a matching piece of interfacing and lining. Baste the interfacing to the wrong side of the embroidery. With right sides facing, stitch the lining to the embroidery making a 1 cm (½ in) seam. Turn right side out and iron lightly. For the tieback, fold the raw edges inside and slipstitch in place. Apply Velcro touch-and-close fastener to secure the ends together. For the lampshade trim, fold the raw edges at one end to the wrong side. Slipstitch or glue the embroidery around the bottom edge of the lampshade, slipping the raw edges inside the folded edge. Slipstitch to secure.

CURTAIN

Measure your window and make a curtain using an evenweave fabric; the curtain should not be very full. Hem the bottom edge of the curtain, but not the sides. Overcast the raw edges. Begin working a border design in the exact centre of the fabric, just above the hem. Work outward to each side edge. When finished, hem the side edges of the curtain. Gently press the finished embroidery.

FOR THE KITCHEN AND DINING ROOM

POTHOLDER

Cut a piece of evenweave fabric about 18–23 cm (7–9 in) square. Overcast the raw edges. Select a design that will fit nicely on the fabric and embroider the design in the centre. Gently iron the finished embroidery. Trim off the overcast edges, then cut padding and a back to the same size; use two to three layers of cotton or wool padding (do not use polyester). Sandwich the padding between the embroidery and the back; baste the edges together. Use bias binding to finish the edges of the potholder, allowing the excess binding at one corner to make a hanging loop.

SHELF BORDER

Cut evenweave fabric slightly longer than your shelf and wide enough for the design plus 1 cm (½ in). Overcast the raw edges. Embroider a border design along the centre of the fabric. Gently press the finished embroidery. Trim off the overcast edges. Cut a matching piece of interfacing to the wrong side of the embroidery. Fold the raw edges of the embroidery 6 mm (¼ in) to the wrong side and secure to the interfacing with small slipstitches.

Iron lightly. Pin or glue the border to the front of your cupboard shelf.

RECTANGULAR TABLE LINEN

Cut a piece of evenweave fabric 2.5 cm (1 in) larger all around than the desired finished size of the item (tablecloth, centrepiece, placemat, plate liner, traycloth or doily). Overcast the raw edges. Decide where you wish to place the design. Embroider the design, adding a border all around the item if

desired. Carefully iron the finished embroidery. Cut away excess fabric, leaving 2 cm (¾ in) for hemming. Fold the fabric 6 mm (¼ in) to the wrong side, then fold the fabric again, this time 1 cm (½ in) to the wrong side. Baste, then sew the hem in place with small slipstitches. Iron gently.

ROUND TABLECLOTH OR CENTREPIECE

Calculate the finished size of your design using the formula on page 8; cut evenweave fabric 3.5 cm (1½ in) larger than the calculated size all round. Overcast the raw edges. Find the exact centre of the fabric and the design; mark on the fabric with a basting thread. Count from the centre of the graph and the fabric to start the design. Work the graph, which is one-quarter of the design. Then turn the fabric clockwise and work the next quarter. Continue turning and repeating the quarter pattern twice more until the design is finished. Carefully iron the embroidery. Measure 3 cm (1¼ in) away from the outer edge of the embroidery and trim off the excess fabric. Fold the fabric 6 mm (¼ in) to the wrong side twice. Baste, then sew hem in place with small slipstitches. Finish by ironing gently.

ROUND DOILY OR TRAYCLOTH

Work as for the tablecloth, but cut your evenweave fabric 2.5 cm (1 in) larger than the calculated size of the project all round.

EGG COSY

Cut two pieces of evenweave fabric, 2.5 cm (1 in) larger all around than the desired finished size of the egg cosy. Overcast the raw edges. Decide where you wish to place the design, then embroider it on both pieces of fabric. Iron the embroidery carefully. Cut two pieces of iron-on interfacing the same size as the embroidered fabric and iron one to the back of each piece of fabric. Cut away the excess fabric and, with right sides facing, machine stitch the two pieces together, leaving the lower edge open. Turn right side out, turn in the lower edges and catch down with small slipstitches. Stitch cord in place around the seam.

NAPKIN RING

Cut a piece of evenweave fabric about 9 × 15 cm (3½ × 5¼ in). Overcast the raw edges. Embroider a small motif or border design on the fabric. Iron the embroidery carefully and trim away the overcast edges. With right sides facing, place the short ends together and slipstitch in place. Fold the long edges over to the wrong side, the desired number of threads away from the embroidery, overlap slightly and slipstitch together. Turn the napkin ring right side out.

SIX-STRAND EMBROIDERY FLOSS CONVERSION CHART

Key:　　T = Possible substitute　　* = Close match　　— = No match

DMC	Royal Mouliné	Bates/Anchor	DMC	Royal Mouliné	Bates/Anchor	DMC	Royal Mouliné	Bates/Anchor	DMC	Royal Mouliné	Bates/Anchor	DMC	Royal Mouliné	Bates/Anchor	DMC	Royal Mouliné	Bates/Anchor
White	1001	2	437	8200*	362	680	6260*	901	816	2530	44*	936	5260T	269	3326	2115*	25*
Ecru	8600	926	444	6155*	291	699	5375	923*	817	2415T	19	937	5260	268	3328	2045	11*
208	3335*	110*	445	6000	288	700	5365*	229	818	2505*	48	938	8430	381	3340	—	329
209	3415*	105	451	—	399*	701	5365*	227	819	2000	892*	939	4405	127	3341	—	328
210	3320*	104	452	—	399*	702	5330	239	820	4345	134	943	4935*	188*	3345	5025T	268*
211	3410	108*	453	1015T	397*	703	5320	238	822	8605*	387*	945	8020*	347*	3346	5220T	257*
221	2570	897*	469	5255	267*	704	5310*	256*	823	4400*	150	946	7230*	332*	3347	5210*	266*
223	2555	894	470	5255*	267	712	8600*	387*	824	4225	164*	947	7255*	330*	3348	5270*	265
224	2545	893	471	5245	266*	718	3015*	88	825	4215	162*	948	8070	778*	3350	2220	42*
225	2540	892	472	5240	264*	720	—	326	826	4210	161*	950	8020T	4146	3354	2210	74*
300	8330	352*	498	2425T	20*	721	—	324*	827	4605	159*	951	8020T	366*	3362	—	862*
301	8315*	349*	500	5125	879*	722	—	323*	828	4850	158*	954	5455*	203*	3363	—	861*
304	2415*	47*	501	5120*	878	725	6215	306*	829	5825	906	955	5450	206*	3364	—	843*
307	6005*	289*	502	5110	876	726	6150*	295	830	5825*	889*	956	2170*	40*	3371	8435	382
309	2525*	42*	503	5105	875	727	6135	293	831	5825T	889*	957	2160T	40*	3607	—	87*
310	1002	403	504	5100	213*	729	6255	890	832	5815	907	958	—	187	3608	—	86
311	4275T	149*	517	—	169*	730	—	924*	833	5815*	874*	959	—	186	3609	—	85
312	—	147*	518	4860*	168*	731	—	281*	834	5810*	874	961	2515*	76*	3685	2335	70*
315	3130	896*	519	4855T	167*	732	5925T	281*	838	8425*	380	962	2515	76*	3687	2325	69*
316	3120	895*	520	—	862*	733	—	280*	839	8560	380*	963	2505	49*	3688	2320	66*
317	1030*	400*	522	—	859*	734	—	279*	840	8555	379*	964	—	185	3689	2310	49
318	1020*	399*	523	—	859*	738	8245*	942	841	8550	378*	966	5150*	214*	3705	—	35*
319	5025	246*	524	—	858*	739	8240*	885*	842	8505	376*	970	7040	316*	3706	—	28*
320	5015	216*	535	1115T	401*	740	7045	316*	844	1115T	401*	971	7045	316*	3708	—	26*
321	2415	47	543	8500	933*	741	6125	304	869	8720*	944*	972	6120*	298	48	9000*	1201*
322	—	978*	550	3380*	102*	742	6120	303	890	5025*	879*	973	6015	290	51	9014	1220
326	2530*	59*	552	3370*	101	743	6210	297	891	2135	35*	975	8365	355*	52	9006	1208
327	3365*	101*	553	3360	98	744	6110*	301*	892	2130	28	976	8355	308*	53	—	—
333	—	119	554	3355*	96*	745	6105	300*	893	2125*	27	977	8350	307*	57	9002	1203
334	4250T	145	561	—	212*	746	6100	386*	894	2115T	26	986	5430	246*	61	9013T	1218*
335	2525T	42*	562	—	210*	747	4850	158*	895	5430*	246*	987	5020T	244*	62	9000T	1201*
336	4270*	149*	563	—	208*	754	8075	778*	898	8425*	360	988	5295T	243*	67	—	1211*
340	—	118	564	—	203*	758	8080	868	899	2515	27*	989	5405T	242*	69	—	1218*
341	—	117	580	5935	267*	760	2035	9*	900	7230*	333	991	5165T	189*	75	9002	1206*
347	2425*	13*	581	5925	266*	761	2030	8*	902	—	72*	992	4925*	187*	90	9012*	1217
349	2400	13	597	4860*	168*	762	1010*	397*	904	5295*	258*	993	4915*	186*	91	9008*	1211
350	2045T	11	598	4855*	167*	772	—	264*	905	5295	258*	995	4710	410	92	9011T	1216*
351	2015T	11*	600	2225*	59*	775	4600*	128*	906	5285*	256*	996	4700	433	93	9007*	1210*
352	2015	10*	601	2225*	78*	776	2110*	24*	907	5280*	255	3011	5525T	845*	94	9011*	1216
353	2020*	8*	602	2640*	77*	778	3110	968*	909	5370	229	3012	5525*	844*	95	9006T	1208*
355	8095	5968	603	2720*	76*	780	8215*	310*	910	5370*	228*	3013	5515	842*	99	9005T	1207*
356	8090	5975*	604	2710	75*	781	8215	309*	911	5465*	205*	3021	—	382*	101	9009*	1213*
367	5020	216*	605	2155	50*	782	6230	308	912	5465	205	3022	—	8581*	102	—	1208*
368	5005*	240*	606	7260	335	783	6220*	307	913	5460*	209	3023	—	8581*	103	—	1210*
369	5005	213*	608	7255	333*	791	4165*	941*	915	3030	89*	3024	1100	900*	104	9012	1217
370	—	889*	610	5825T	889*	792	4155T	940	917	3020*	89*	3031	—	905*	105	9013*	1218
371	—	888*	611	5735T	898	793	4155	121	918	8330*	341*	3032	8620T	903*	106	9002T	1203*
372	—	887*	612	8815*	832	794	4145	120*	919	8095*	341*	3033	8610*	388*	107	9003	1204
400	8325*	351	613	5605*	956*	796	4340	133*	920	8060*	339*	3041	3215*	871	108	9014*	1220*
402	8305*	347*	632	8530	936*	797	4265*	132*	921	8060T	349*	3042	3205*	869	111	—	1218*
407	8005	882*	640	8625	903	798	4325	131*	922	8315*	324*	3045	6260T	373*	112	9003T	1204*
413	1025*	401	642	8620*	392	799	4250*	130*	924	4830T	851*	3046	5810	887*	113	9007*	1210*
414	1020*	400*	644	8800	830	800	4310	128	926	4820*	779*	3047	5805	886*	114	9010	1215
415	1015	398	645	1115	905*	801	8405	357*	927	4810T	849*	3051	5530T	846*	115	9004	1206
420	8720*	375*	646	1115*	8581	806	4870T	169*	928	1010T	900*	3052	5060*	859*	121	9007	1210
422	8710*	373*	647	1110	8581*	807	4860*	168*	930	4510	922*	3053	5055*	859*	122	9010T	1215*
433	8265	371*	648	1100*	900	809	4145*	130*	931	4505	921*	3064	8005*	914*	123	—	1213*
434	8215*	309	666	2405	46	813	4610*	160*	932	4500	920*	3072	4805*	397*	124	9007T	1210*
435	8210*	369*	676	6250	891	814	2340T	44*	934	5070T	862*	3078	6130	292*	125	9009	1213
436	8205	363*	677	—	886*	815	2530*	43	935	5225T	862*	3325	4200	159*	126	9006*	1208*

2

THE
VIKING AGE

The Vikings were ancestors to all three Scandinavian peoples, and left behind them a fascinating artistic heritage.

In this chapter, as well as patterns culled from fifth-century textiles, I have included a wall-hanging based

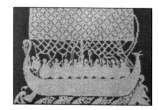

on a complex bas-relief carved in limestone from Gotland, Sweden; these

rock carvings may originally have been used as 'nameplates' outside Viking homes. There is also a simpler design, used here to embellish a bookmark,

which has been taken from a decorated sword found in a Viking grave.

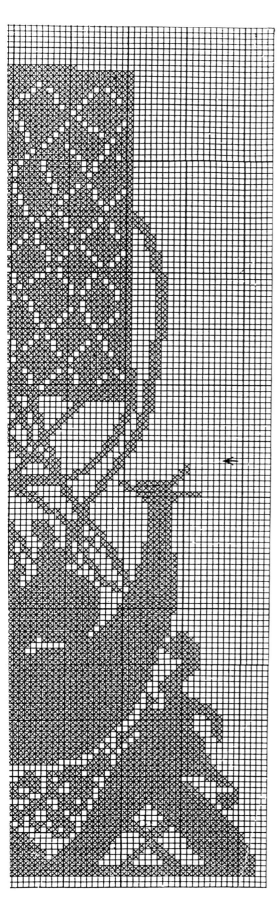

WALLHANGING WITH SHIP

(Based on a bas-relief carved in limestone from Gotland, Sweden, 5th century)

MATERIAL:
blue burlap, 6 threads per cm
(15 threads per in)
CUTTING SIZE:
70 × 65 cm (27½ × 25½ in)
FINISHED SIZE:
58 × 59 cm (22¾ × 23¼ in)
THREAD:
Danish mohair, 2 × 50 g / 1.75 m
(2 oz / 70 in) bundles (pearl
cotton no. 3 or tapestry wool can
be used as a less expensive
alternative)

⊠	white

To finish, measure 10 cm (4 in)
from the embroidery to the top
edge and make a 2.5 cm (1 in)
casing. At the lower edge,
measure 5.5 cm (2¼ in) from
the embroidery and make a
similar casing.

CUSHION WITH VIKING DESIGN

(Based on a design from Väskinde, Sweden, 5th century)

MATERIAL:
brown burlap, 6 threads per cm
(15 threads per in)

CUTTING SIZE:
65 × 65 cm (25½ × 25½ in)

FINISHED SIZE:
58 × 58 cm (22¾ × 22¾ in)

THREAD:
Danish mohair, 1 × 50 g / 1.75 m
(2 oz / 70 in) bundle (pearl cotton
no. 3 or tapestry wool can be
used as a less expensive
alternative)

⊠	black
⊟	black (backstitch)

See page 13 for instructions on
making a cushion.

CHAIR COVER WITH VIKING KNOT AND BORDER

(Based on a Swedish design, 5th century)

MATERIAL:
beige burlap, 6 threads per cm
(15 threads per in)

CUTTING SIZE:
57 × 120 cm (22½ × 47 in)

FINISHED SIZE:
52 × 115 cm (20½ × 45¼ in)

THREAD:
Danish mohair, 1 × 50 g / 1.75 m
(2 oz / 70 in) bundle (pearl cotton
no. 3 or tapestry wool can be
used as a less expensive
alternative)

■	black
⊟	black (backstitch)

Shrink the fabric in warm water
before stitching the embroidery.
The simplest method for making
the cover is to stitch the fabric
into a 'bag' to hold the foam
cushions, inserting a zipper in the
lower seam to close. This can be
tucked out of sight beneath the
seat cushion.

BENCH COVER WITH BIRDS

*(Based on a tapestry from Baldishol church, Norway,
about 12th century)*

MATERIAL:
orange burlap, 6 threads per cm
(15 threads per in)
CUTTING SIZE:
45 cm (18 in) deep × length
required
FINISHED SIZE:
39 cm (15½ in) deep approx
THREAD:
DMC embroidery floss. Use 4
strands in the needle

◣	820	dark blue
⧄	518	turquoise
⊠	989	green
⌞	833	gold
◺	822	light beige

This cushion can be attached
with simple 2 cm (¾ in) ties or, if
the bench is very large, velcro
strips may be more suitable.

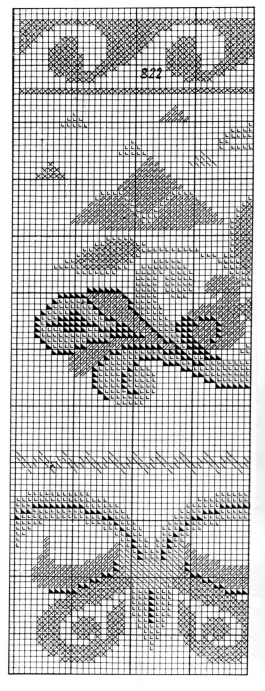

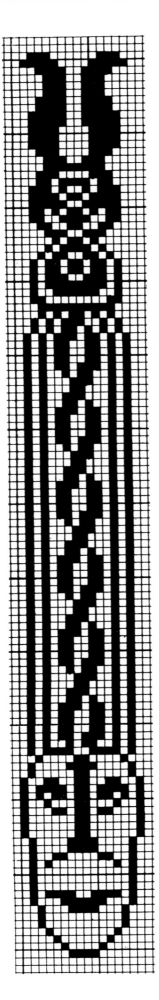

BOOKMARK WITH VIKING DESIGN

(Based on a design from a sword found in a Swedish Viking grave, about 5th century)

MATERIAL:
linen, 10 threads per cm
(25 threads per in)

CUTTING SIZE:
10 × 30 cm (4 × 11¾ in)

FINISHED SIZE:
4 × 27 cm (1¾ × 10¾ in) approx

THREAD:
DMC embroidery floss. Use 2
strands in the needle

◼	796	dark blue

See page 10 for instructions on
making a bookmark.

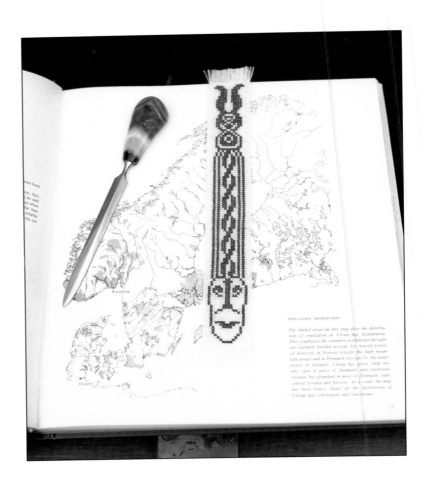

3
DESIGNS FROM
NORWAY

The rugged countryside of Norway lends itself perfectly to the keeping of goats, and the country is well-known for its beautiful traditional knitting designs worked in natural wools. These patterns, many inspired by the beautiful Norwegian scenery, lend themselves equally well to  embroidery, and a number of these designs, from simple to complex, are included in this chapter. Others have been adapted  from woven or embroidered museum pieces, including 'primitive' representations of animals which date from about 1700.

As well as complete designs, I have also provided a selection of traditional motifs and borders which can be used in a variety of ways to create your own original items. Taken together, this diverse collection of designs, both large and small, should provide something to suit every taste and level of stitching skill.

DECORATIVE WALLHANGING

(Based on a Norwegian woven wall carpet, 17th century)

MATERIAL:
linen, 8 threads per cm
(20 threads per in)

CUTTING SIZE:
45 × 55 cm (18 × 21½ in)

FINISHED SIZE:
35 × 45 cm (13¾ × 18 in)

THREAD:
DMC embroidery floss. Use 3
strands in the needle

◣	433	brown
∕	921	rust
∙	353	light salmon
⋀	760	dark rose
⠇⠇⠇	906	green
⟍	472	light green
●	517	blue
⌐	597	turquoise
⊟		white
⊠	734	gold
⊟	433	brown (backstitch)

See page 12 for instructions on
making a wallhanging.

CUSHION AND BORDER WITH REINDEER

CUSHION

MATERIAL:
blue Aida, 4½ stitches per cm
(11 stitches per in)

CUTTING SIZE:
50 × 50 cm (19½ × 19½ in)

FINISHED SIZE:
45 × 45 cm (18 × 18 in) approx

THREAD:
DMC embroidery floss and pearl
cotton no. 8. Use 1 strand of pearl
cotton in the needle and 3 strands
of floss

BORDER

MATERIAL:
beige Aida, 5½ stitches per cm
(13½ stitches per in)

CUTTING SIZE:
12 cm (4¾ in) deep × length
required

FINISHED SIZE:
7 cm (2¾ in) deep

THREAD:
Use 2 strands of pearl cotton

Work the border from the section
of the chart indicated by the 4
small arrows, repeating as many
times as necessary to fit the
length required.

☒	white (pearl cotton)
◤	891 red

☒	797 blue
◤	891 red

CURTAIN WITH REINDEER AND TREES

MATERIAL:
beige Aida, 4½ stitches per cm
(11 stitches per in)

CUTTING SIZE:
45 cm (18 in) deep × length
required

FINISHED SIZE:
39 cm (15½ in)

THREAD:
DMC embroidery floss. Use 3
strands in the needle

⊠	938 brown

Make hems of 2 cm (¾ in) on the
bottom edge and 1 cm (½ in) on
the other 3 sides. Stitch the
embroidery 3 cm (1¼ in) from the
lower edge.

A tassled ribbon gives a nice
finish to the curtain. Baste it
loosely along the bottom edge
and machine stitch into place.

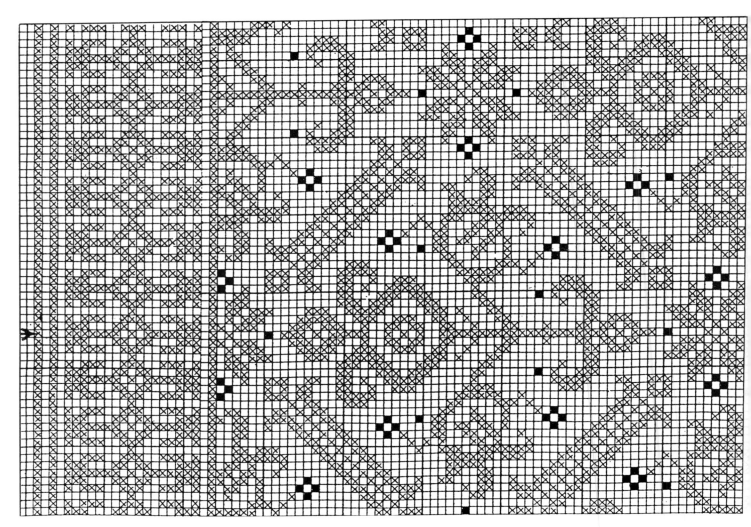

CUSHION WITH ABSTRACT FLOWERS

(Based on a design from Gudbrandsdalen, Norway, about 1700)

MATERIAL:
beige Aida, 4½ stitches per cm
(11 stitches per in)
CUTTING SIZE:
50 × 45 cm (19½ × 18 in)
FINISHED SIZE:
45 × 40 cm (18 × 15¾ in)
approx

ZIPPER:
30 cm (11¾ in)
THREAD:
DMC embroidery floss. Use 3
strands in the needle

⊠	3328	red
■	932	light blue

See page 13 for instructions on
making a cushion.

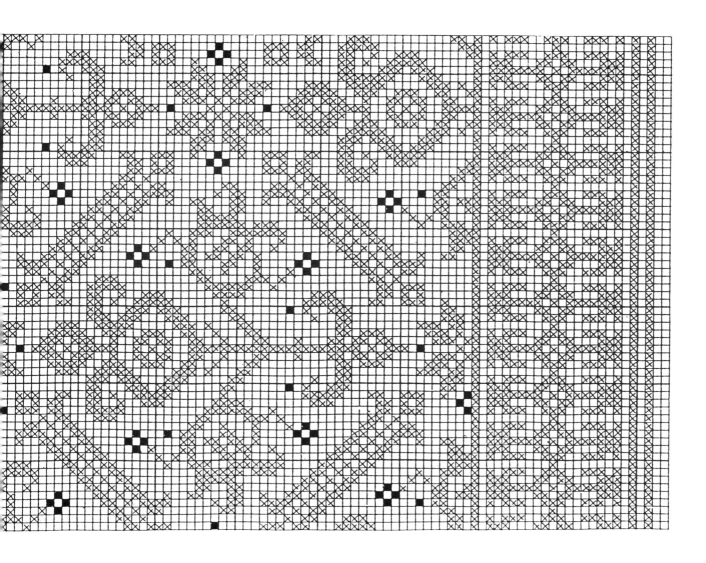

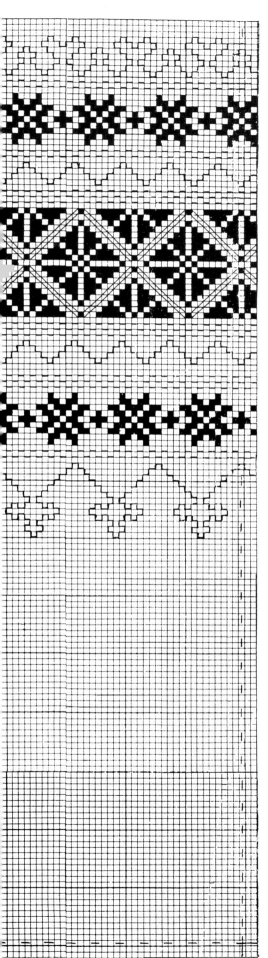

TABLECLOTH WITH
TRADITIONAL BORDERS

(Based on an embroidery from Saude, Telemark, Norway)

MATERIAL:
linen, 8 threads per cm
(20 threads per in)

CUTTING SIZE:
1 × 1 m (39½ × 39½ in)

FINISHED SIZE:
80 × 80 cm (31½ × 31½ in)

THREAD:
DMC black pearl cotton no. 8
(approximately 5 balls)

■	black
⊟	black (backstitch)

Finish with a 2 cm (¾ in) hem.

TABLE CENTREPIECE WITH TRADITIONAL BORDERS

(Based on an embroidery from Saude, Telemark, Norway)

MATERIAL:
linen, 8 threads per cm
(20 threads per in)

CUTTING SIZE:
50 × 50 cm (19½ × 19½ in)

FINISHED SIZE:
41 × 41 cm (16 × 16 in)

THREAD:
DMC pearl cotton no. 8

■ 310 black

□ 310 black (backstitch)

See page 14 for instructions on making a table centrepiece.

PASTEL REPEATS

(Based on a design from Gudbrandsdalen, Norway, 17th century)

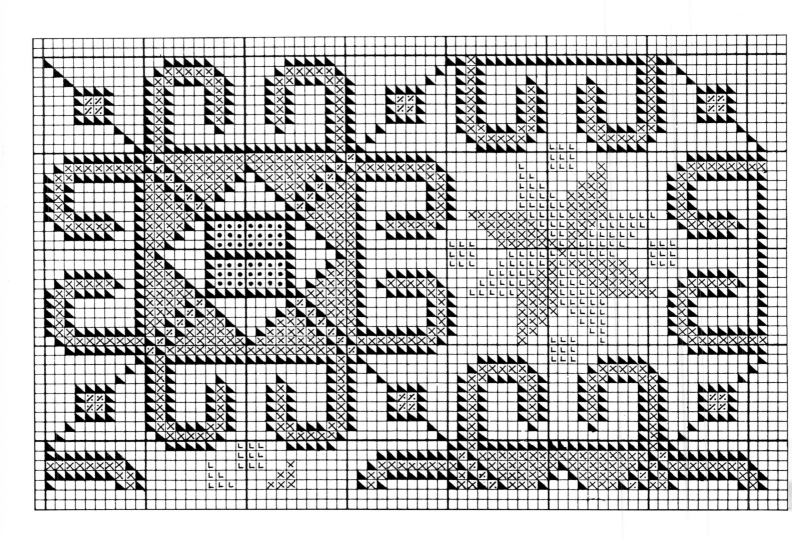

MATERIAL:
rose Aida, 5 stitches per cm
(12½ stitches per in)

DESIGN SIZE:
15.5 x 18.5 cm (6 x 7¼ in)

THREAD:
DMC embroidery floss. Use 2
strands in the needle

◣	3021	brown
⊠	648	grey
L		white
⊙	722	rust
⊡	743	yellow

This design could also be used to
cover a footstool or to make a
cushion.

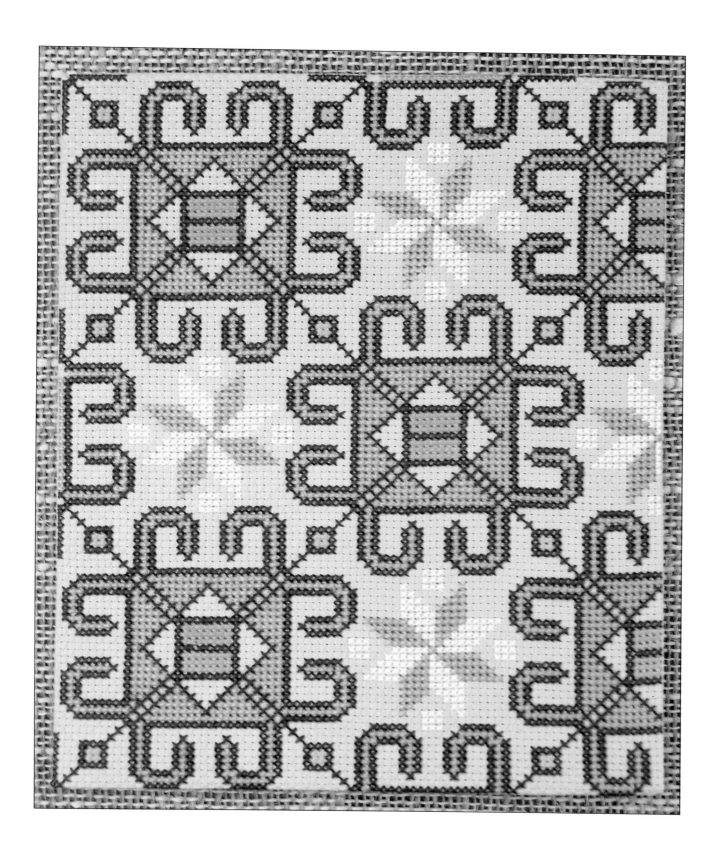

COOL BLUE REPEATS

(Based on a Norwegian design, about 17th century)

MATERIAL:
light blue pearl Aida, 3½ stitches
per cm (8½ stitches per in) approx
DESIGN SIZE:
27 × 30 cm (10¾ × 11¾ in)
THREAD:
DMC embroidery floss. Use 3
strands in the needle

⊠	797 blue

The design could also be worked
on canvas using tapestry wool,
and used to cover a footstool or
similar piece of furniture.

WALLHANGING WITH NORWEGIAN FOLK COSTUME

MATERIAL:
linen, 10 threads per cm
(25 threads per in)
CUTTING SIZE:
35 × 55 cm (13¾ × 21½ in)

FINISHED SIZE:
27 × 42 cm (10¾ × 16½ in)
approx
THREAD:
DMC embroidery floss. Use 2
strands in the needle

Make the hems on the long sides
8 threads deep. Measure 3 cm
(1¼ in) from the top and bottom
of the embroidery and make the
casings for the fittings.

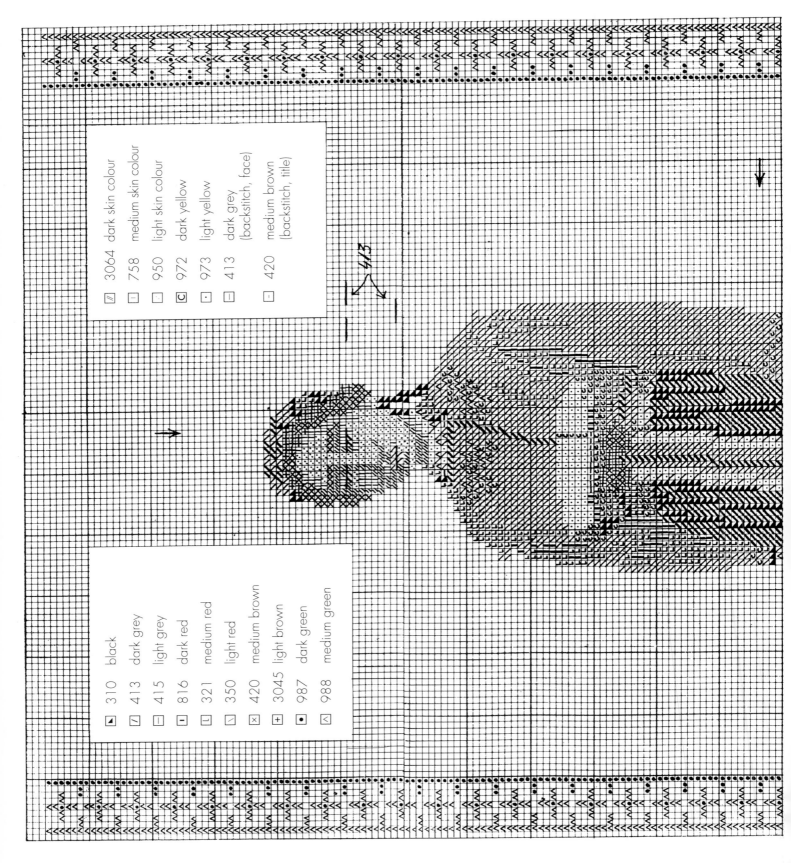

	3064	dark skin colour
▨		
−	758	medium skin colour
⋅	950	light skin colour
C	972	dark yellow
•	973	light yellow
−	413	dark grey (backstitch, face)
−	420	medium brown (backstitch, title)

4/3

◣	310	black
⊿	413	dark grey
⊟	415	light grey
−	816	dark red
⌐	321	medium red
⧄	350	light red
×	420	medium brown
+	3045	light brown
●	987	dark green
◁	988	medium green

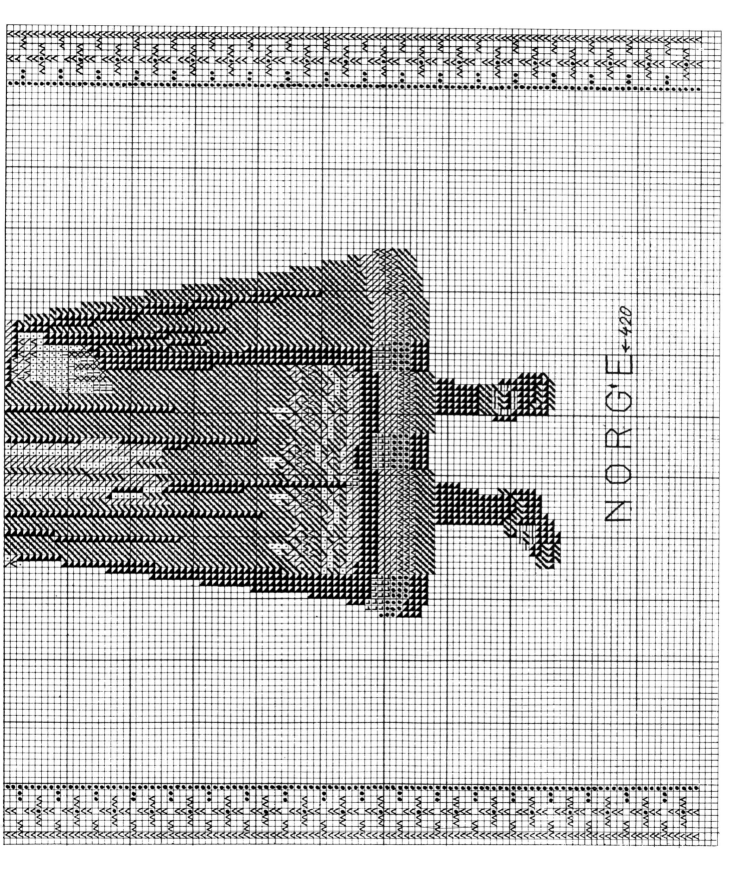

STYLIZED FLOWER PATTERN

(Based on a Norwegian design, 17th–18th century)

MATERIAL:
Needlepoint canvas, 5 stitches per cm (12½ stitches per in)

DESIGN SIZE:
21 × 26 cm (8¼ × 10¼ in)

THREAD:
DMC embroidery floss. Use all 6 strands in the needle

■	938	dark brown
□		white
⌊	729	gold
◺	470	green
⊡	3328	red
⊔	3354	rose
●	518	blue
∧	598	light blue
⊏	3328	red (backstitch)

The design can be used to cover a footstool or similar piece of furniture.

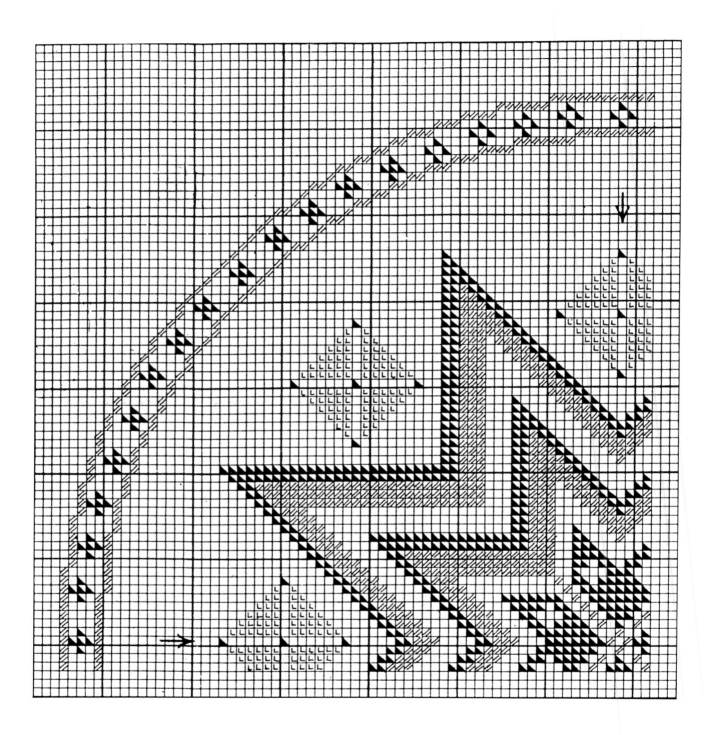

TABLE CENTREPIECE
WITH NORWEGIAN DESIGN

MATERIAL:
white Aida, 4½ stitches per cm
(11 stitches per in)

CUTTING SIZE:
40 × 40 cm (15¾ × 15¾ in)

FINISHED SIZE:
34 × 34 cm (13½ × 13½ in)

BIAS TAPE:
red, 1.15 m (43 in)

THREAD:
DMC embroidery floss. Use 3
strands in the needle

▨	351	red
◣	798	blue
L	894	rose

Once the excess fabric has been
trimmed away baste and then
machine stitch the bias tape in
place.

TABLE RUNNER WITH NORWEGIAN DESIGN

(Based on a design from Setesdalen, Norway, 17th century)

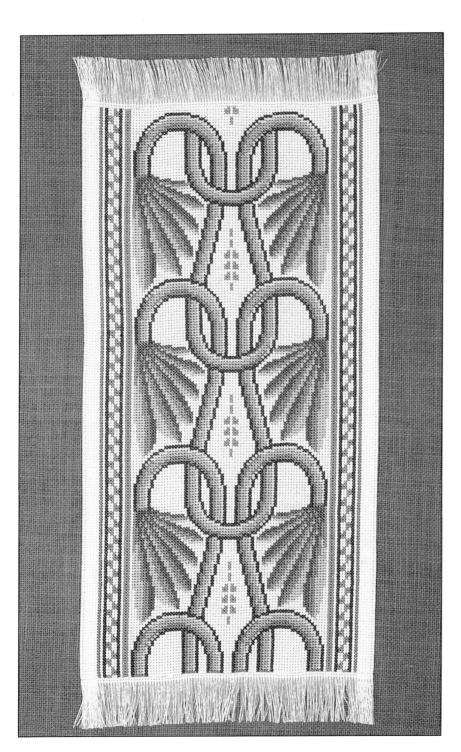

MATERIAL:
beige Aida, 4½ stitches per cm
(11 stitches per in)
CUTTING SIZE:
30 cm (11¾ in) × length required
FINISHED SIZE:
25 cm (9¾ in)
THREAD:
DMC embroidery floss. Use 3
strands in the needle

◣	3021	dark brown
▨	3022	medium grey
◸	648	light grey
▢	3072	lightest grey
◺	580	dark green
✕	581	medium green
◻	472	light green
⦿	921	rust

Once the runner has been sewn
to the length required, machine
stitch along the last row of cross
stitching to hold the material in
shape. Measure 3.5 cm (1¼ in) to
make a fringe and trim away
excess fabric.

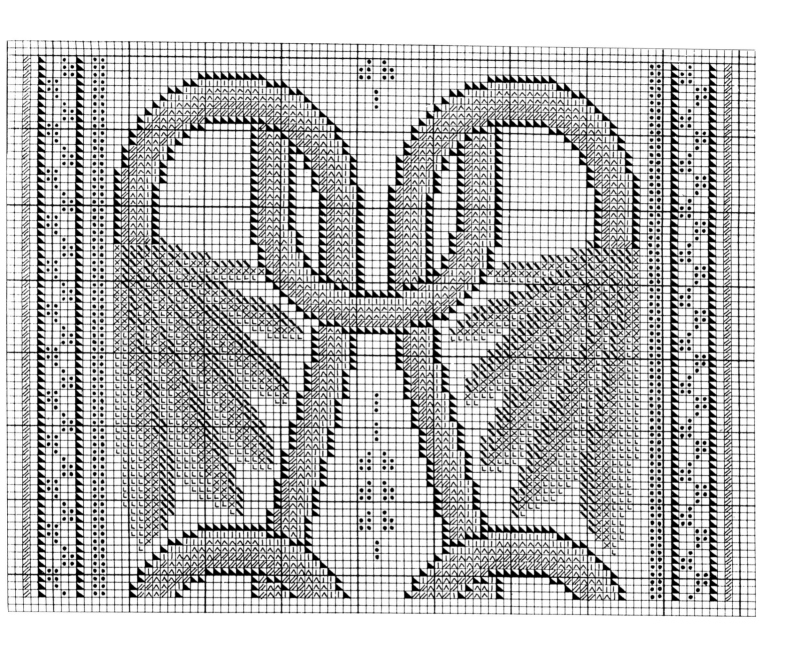

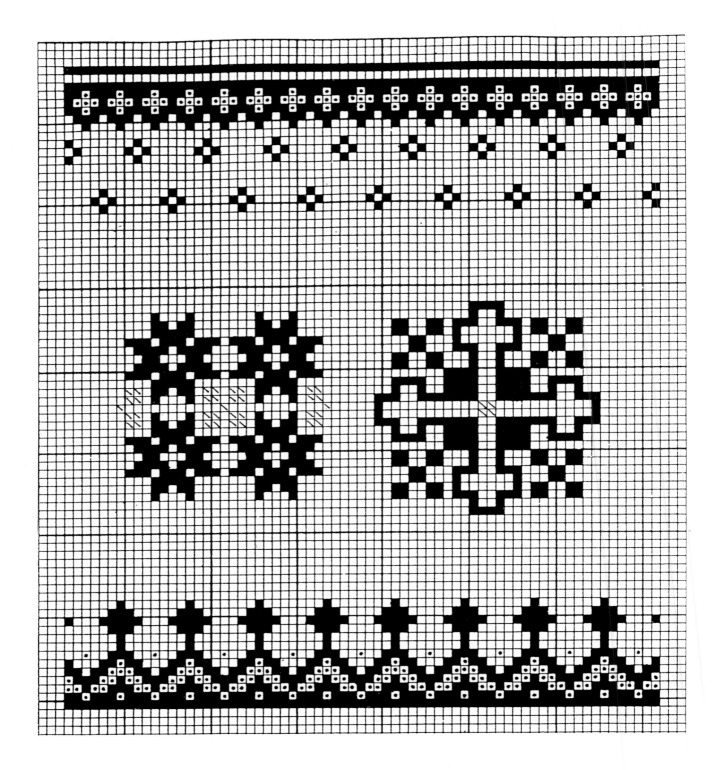

NORWEGIAN MOTIFS AND BORDERS I

MATERIAL:
Samples worked on pearl Aida, 7½ stitches per cm (18½ stitches per in), stitching over 2 threads at a time

DESIGN SIZE:
19 × 22 cm (17½ × 8¾ in)

THREAD:
DMC embroidery floss. Use 3 strands in the needle

■	797	blue
●	349	red
╲		white

These motifs and border designs are suitable for a tablecloth, centrepiece, placemat or table runner.

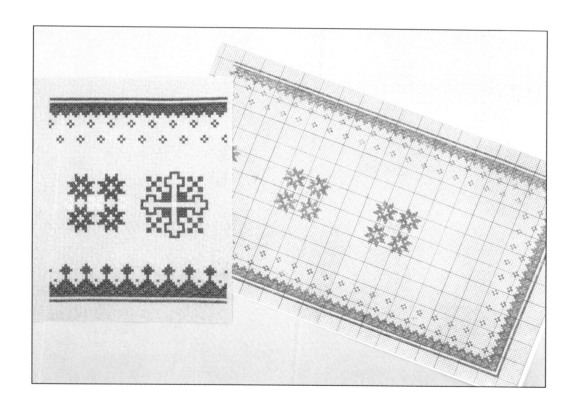

NORWEGIAN MOTIFS AND BORDERS II

MATERIAL:
Samples worked on linen, 8
threads per cm (20 threads per in)
DESIGN SIZE:
16 x 20.5 cm (6¼ x 8 in)
THREAD:
DMC embroidery floss. Use 3
strands in the needle

◾ 336 dark blue

◉ 415 grey

These motifs and border designs
are suitable for a tablecloth,
centrepiece, placemat or table
runner.

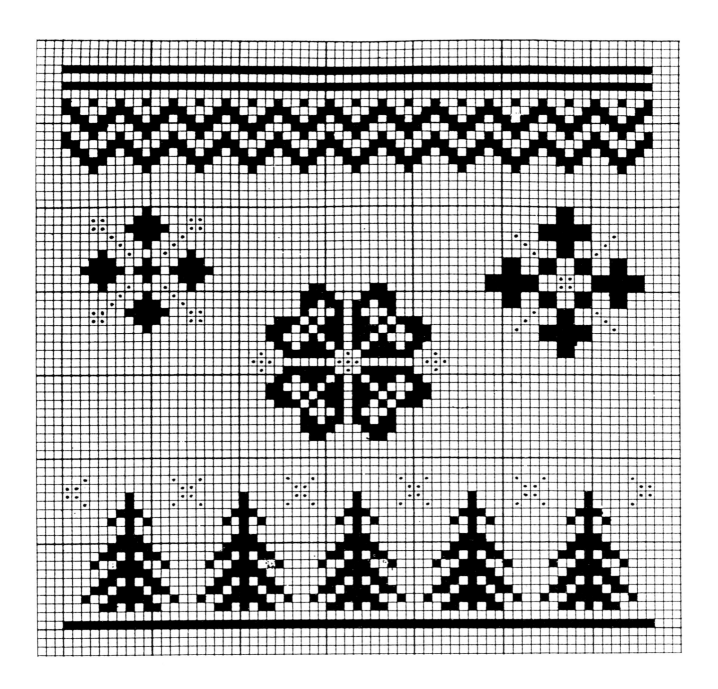

BLOCKS AND BANDS

(Based on a design from Oppdal Trøndelag, Norway, 17th century)

MATERIAL:
light beige Aida, 4½ stitches per cm (11 stitches per in)

DESIGN SIZE:
29 × 35 cm (11½ × 13¾ in)

THREAD:
DMC embroidery floss. Use 4 strands in the needle

■	938	brown
⊠	783	gold
⊡	807	turquoise
L	827	light turquoise

The design is suitable for making a cushion, tablecloth or table runner.

PICTURE WITH REINDEER AND BIRDS

(Based on a Norwegian design, about 1700)

MATERIAL:
beige Aida, 5½ stitches per cm
(13½ stitches per in)

CUTTING SIZE:
20 × 14 cm (8 × 5½ in)

FINISHED SIZE:
16 × 10 cm (6¼ × 4 in)

PIECE OF CARDBOARD:
16 × 10 cm (6¼ × 4 in)

THREAD:
DMC embroidery floss. Use 2
strands in the needle

▣	610	brown
◣	400	rust
⊡	797	blue
▨	904	green

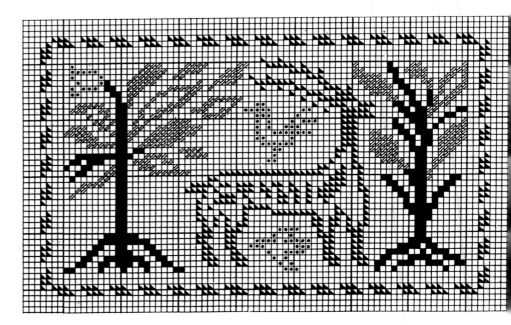

See page 11 for instructions on making an unframed picture.

PICTURE WITH HORSE

(Based on a Norwegian design, about 1700)

MATERIAL:
beige Aida, 5½ stitches per cm
(13½ stitches per in)

CUTTING SIZE:
18 × 16 cm (7 × 6¼ in)

FINISHED SIZE:
15 × 12 cm (5¾ × 4¾ in)

PIECE OF CARDBOARD:
15 × 12 cm (5¾ × 4¾ in)

THREAD:
DMC embroidery floss. Use 2
strands in the needle

| ☑ | 580 | green |
| ◪ | 918 | brown |

See page 11 for instructions on
making an unframed picture.

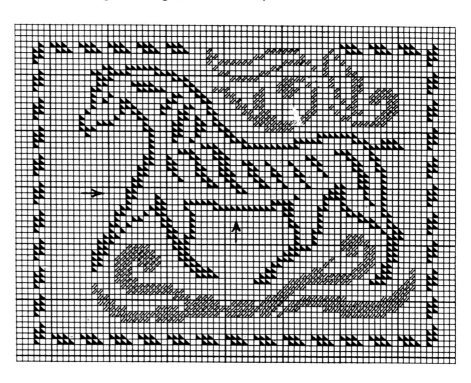

PICTURE WITH LION

(Based on a Norwegian design about 1700)

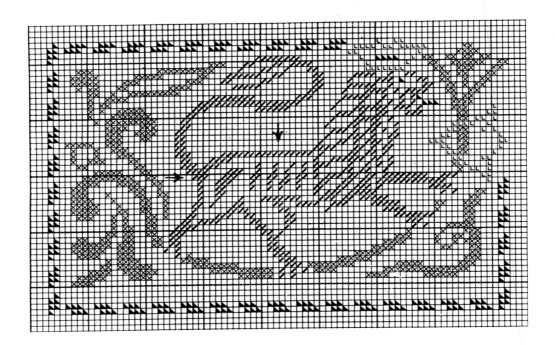

MATERIAL:
beige Aida, 5½ stitches per cm
(13½ stitches per in)
CUTTING SIZE:
21 × 16 cm (8¼ × 6¼ in)
FINISHED SIZE:
17 × 11.5 cm (6¾ × 4½ in)
PIECE OF CARDBOARD:
17 × 11.5 cm (6¾ × 4½ in)
THREAD:
DMC embroidery floss. Use 2
strands in the needle

⁄	797	blue
⊠	912	turquoise
◣	498	red
L	783	yellow

See page 11 for instructions on making an unframed picture.

4
DESIGNS FROM
SWEDEN

Sweden has a gentler, more varied countryside than Norway, and the flora found here is similarly more diverse. The famous botanist Carl von Linné, who first classified plants into families, came from Sweden, and the charming little flower *Linnaea borealis* is named after him. Here a realistic depiction of the plant has been

used to create a pretty table centrepiece and runner, which would add charm to a cottage-style interior. Other plants represented in this collection are the hairy greenweed and oak leaves, the symbol of the Swedish provinces of

Halland and Blekinge respectively.

Other designs have been taken from woven museum pieces or from the beautiful embroidered cushions that were used on long journeys in uncomfortable horse-drawn carriages along the rough forest roads of the country.

Several charming folk art designs are also included, to complete a collection with an overall feeling of lightness and simplicity.

HEARTS AND CROWNS

(Repeating design with Swedish crowns)

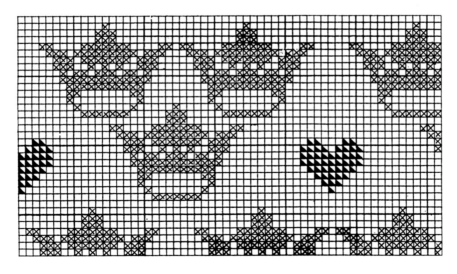

MATERIAL:
blue burlap, 6 threads per cm
(15 threads per in)

DESIGN SIZE:
29 x 34 cm (11½ x 13½ in)

THREAD:
DMC embroidery floss. Use all 6
strands in the needle

◣	720	orange
☒	725	yellow

This design would be suitable for
several of the projects described
in Chapter 1.

WALLHANGING WITH SWEDISH FOLK COSTUME

MATERIAL:
linen, 10 threads per cm
(25 threads per in)
CUTTING SIZE:
35 × 55 cm (13¾ × 21½ in)

FINISHED SIZE:
27 × 42 cm (10¾ × 16½ in)
approx
THREAD:
DMC embroidery floss. Use 2
strands in the needle

Make the hems on the long sides
8 threads deep. Measure 3 cm
(1¼ in) from top and bottom of
the embroidery and make the
casings for the fittings.

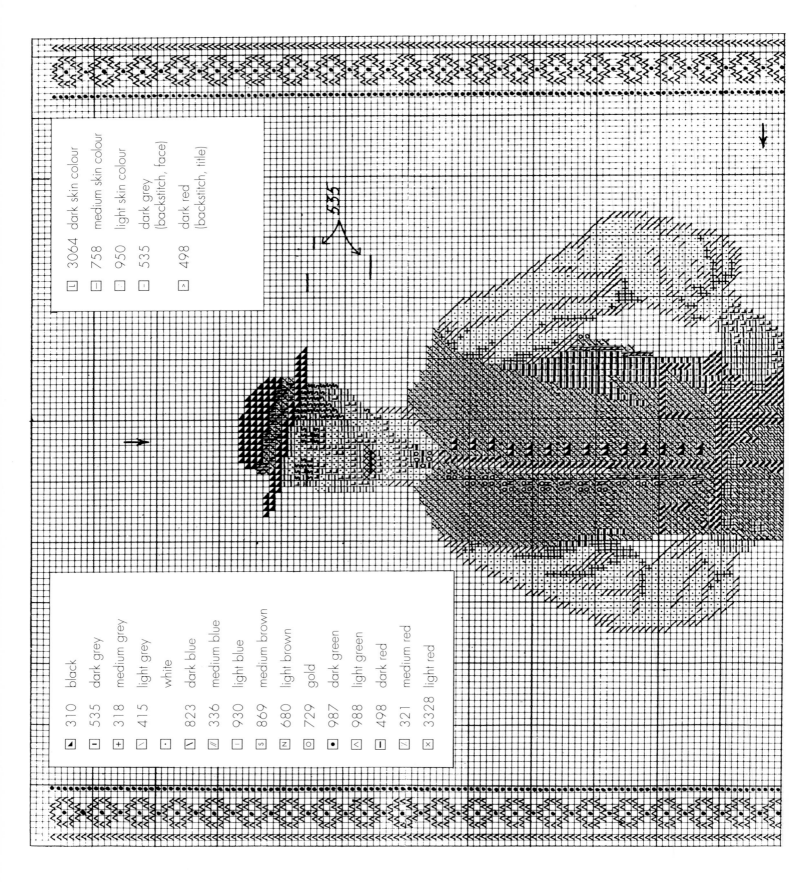

	3064	dark skin colour
□	758	medium skin colour
□	950	light skin colour
□	535	dark grey (backstitch, face)
▷	498	dark red (backstitch, title)

535

◢	310	black
−	535	dark grey
+	318	medium grey
◿	415	light grey
·		white
◺	823	dark blue
◿	336	medium blue
−	930	light blue
s	869	medium brown
z	680	light brown
○	729	gold
●	987	dark green
◁	988	light green
		498	dark red
◿	321	medium red
×	3328	light red

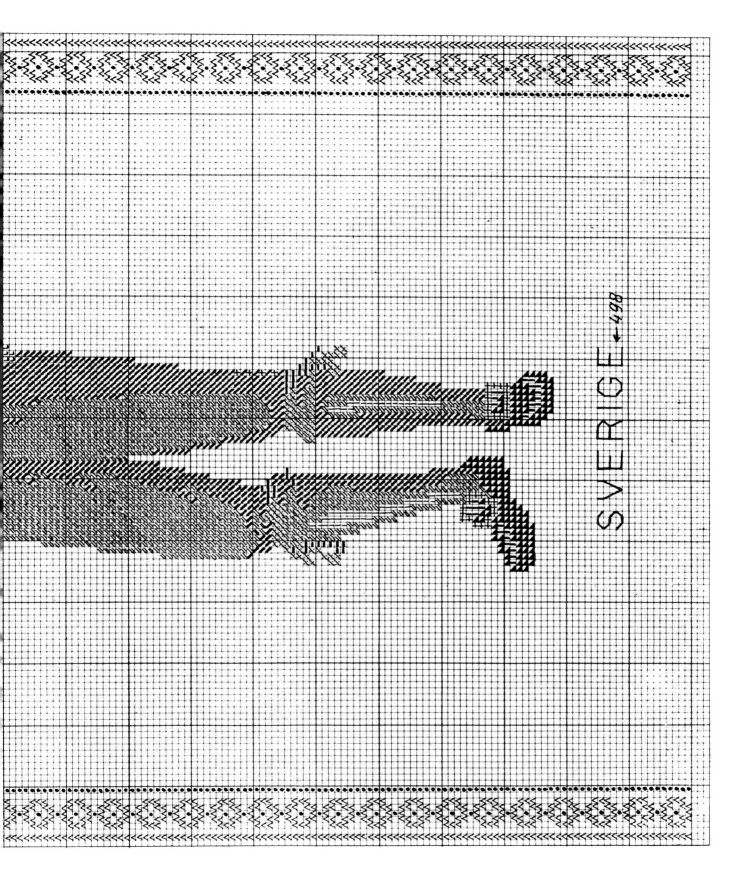

PICTURE WITH
BOWL OF FLOWERS

(Based on an embroidery from Blekinge, Sweden)

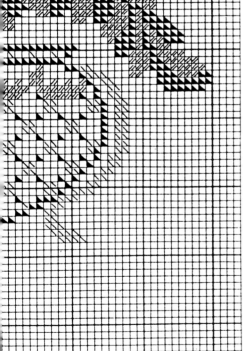

MATERIAL:
light beige Aida, 5½ stitches per
cm (13½ stitches per in)

CUTTING SIZE:
30 × 38 cm (11¾ × 15 in)

FINISHED SIZE:
25 × 32 cm (9¾ × 12½ in)

BIAS TAPE:
1.25 m (49 in)

PIECE OF CARDBOARD:
25 × 32 cm (9¾ × 12½ in)

THREAD:
DMC embroidery floss. Use 2
strands in the needle

◤	824	dark blue
▨	518	light blue
◺	335	red
⊡	894	rose

Iron the embroidery and baste the
bias tape around the edges and
then machine stitch in place,
before securing to the cardboard
in the usual way.

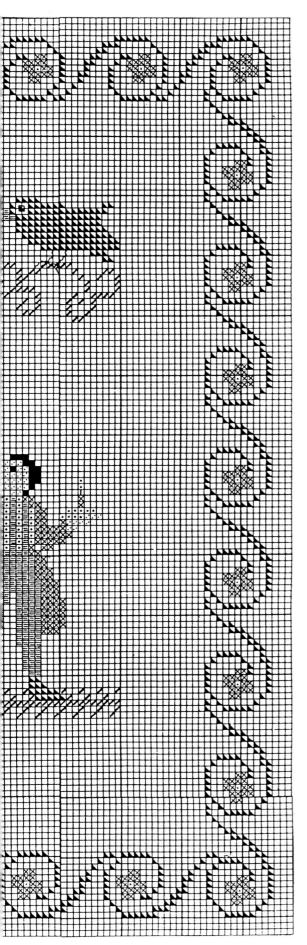

CUSHION WITH FOLK ART DESIGN

(Based on a design from Blekinge, Sweden)

MATERIAL:
linen, 8 threads per cm
(20 threads per in)

CUTTING SIZE:
47 × 52 cm (18½ × 20½ in)

FINISHED SIZE:
41 × 46 cm (16 × 18 in)

THREAD:
DMC embroidery floss. Use 3
strands in the needle

Make the seams for the
cushion 1 cm (½ in) from the
embroidered border.

◪	797	blue
☒	350	red
⊡	3340	salmon
·	725	yellow
■	975	brown
☐	950	skin colour
⊘	904	green
▤	833	gold
⊟	975	brown (backstitch)
⊟	833	gold (backstitch)

TOWEL WITH BIRDS BORDER

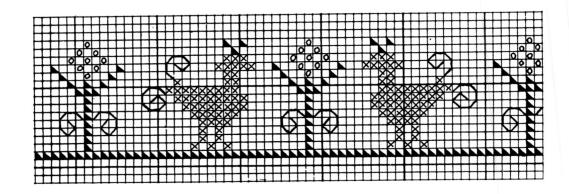

MATERIAL:
white Aida, 4½ stitches per cm
(11 stitches per in)
CUTTING SIZE:
8 cm (3 in) deep × width of towel
FINISHED SIZE:
4.75 cm (1¾ in) deep
THREAD:
DMC embroidery floss. Use 3
strands in the needle

☒	350	red
◣	824	blue
◉	518	light blue
⊟	824	blue (backstitch)

See page 13 for instructions on
making bath towel edging.

CUSHION AND TABLE RUNNER
WITH TULIPS

MATERIAL:
linen, 10 threads per cm
(25 threads per in)

CUSHION
CUTTING SIZE:
40 × 40 cm (15¾ × 15¾ in)
FINISHED SIZE:
35 × 35 cm (13¾ × 13¾ in)
approx

TABLE RUNNER
CUTTING SIZE:
40 × 90 cm (15¾ × 35½ in)
FINISHED SIZE:
32 × 85 cm (12½ × 33½ in)
approx
THREAD:
DMC embroidery floss. Use 2
strands in the needle

◤	869	brown
⊘	3346	dark green
⊠	3347	light green
⊞	350	red
⊡	760	medium red
⊡	353	light red
■	310	black
⊡	312	blue
⊟	869	brown (backstitch)

Use scraps of thread to make
4 tassels and stitch one to each
corner of the finished cushion.
 Work the table runner by
repeating the border of the
cushion, ending each side with a
small tulip and turning the corners
following the chart below.

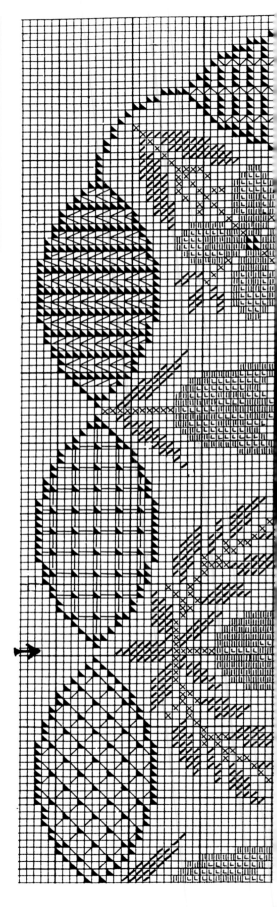

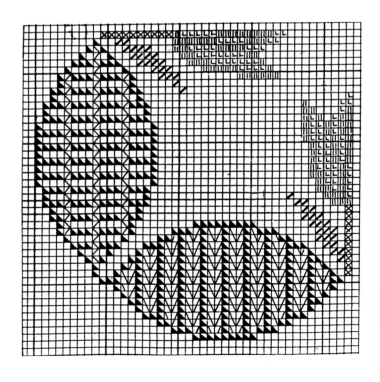

CUSHION WITH HORSEMAN

(Based on a folk art design, Proposal, from Halland, Sweden)

MATERIAL:
beige Aida, 4½ stitches per cm
(11 stitches per in)

CUTTING SIZE:
48 × 48 cm (19 × 19 in)

FINISHED SIZE:
43 × 43 cm (17 × 17 in)

THREAD:
DMC embroidery floss. Use 3
strands in the needle

◣	844	dark coke-grey
⚊	905	green
▨	826	blue
·	680	light brown
L	676	straw
☐	950	rose
⊠	3328	red

See page 13 for instructions on
making a cushion.

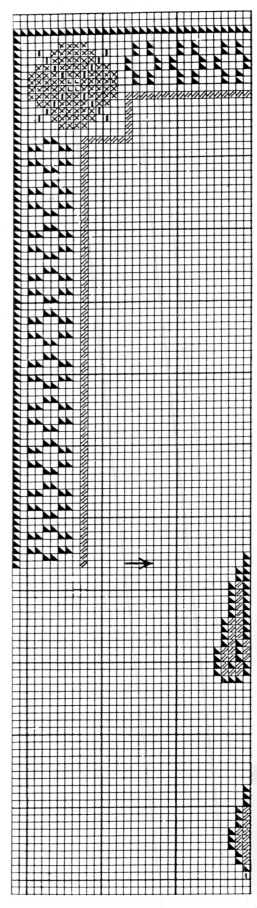

KITCHEN CURTAIN
WITH SWAGGED BORDER

(Based on a design from Blekinge, Sweden)

MATERIAL:
white Aida, 4½ stitches per cm
(11 stitches per in)

CUTTING SIZE:
24 cm (9½ in) deep × length
required

FINISHED SIZE:
18 cm (7 in) deep

THREAD:
DMC embroidery floss. Use 3
strands in the needle

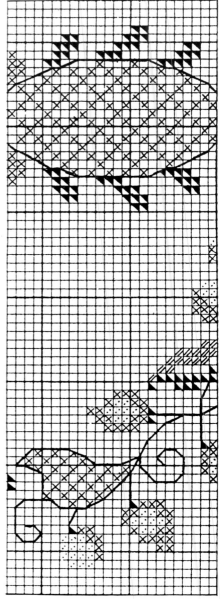

◣	824	dark blue
▨	518	light blue
⊠	351	red
☐	725	yellow
⊟	824	dark blue (backstitch)

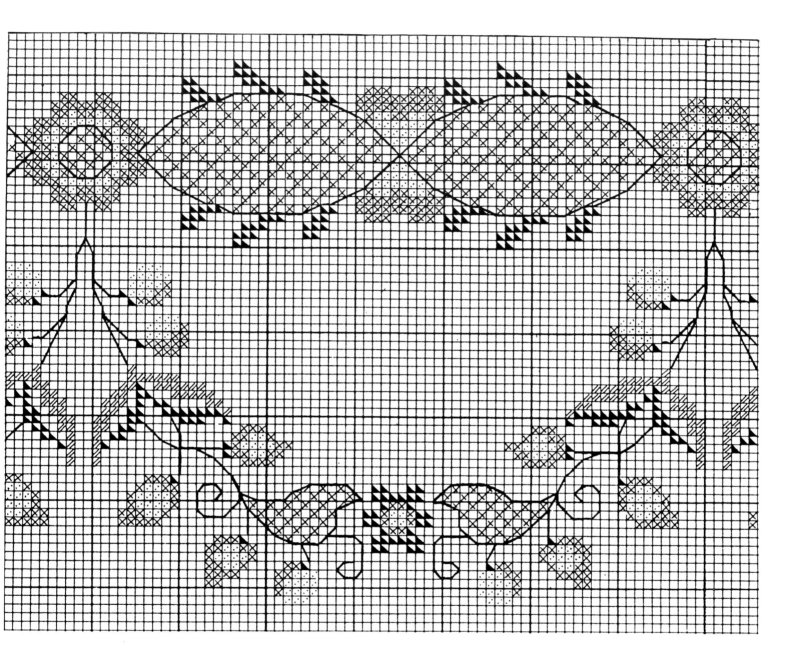

When stitching is complete, count 8 stitches from the top of the embroidery and make a hem 7 stitches deep. Along the bottom, count 7 stitches from the embroidery and make a hem 4 stitches deep. Gather the curtain fabric slightly, baste the embroidery on to it and then machine stitch in place along the top of the curtain.

To make a matching tieback, work repeats of the border as necessary, omitting the swags.

Turn the edges to the wrong side 2 stitches away from the embroidery and slipstitch in place. Sew a curtain ring on each end to fasten the tieback to a hook in the wall.

TABLE CENTREPIECE
WITH BIRDS AND SNOWFLAKES

*(Based on a detail from a woven piece from Bohuslän,
southern Sweden, 19th century)*

MATERIAL:
red Aida, 4½ stitches per cm
(11 stitches per in)

CUTTING SIZE:
33 × 33 cm (13 × 13 in)

FINISHED SIZE:
27.5 × 27.5 cm (11 × 11 in)

THREAD:
DMC embroidery floss. Use 3
strands in the needle

☒	white

See page 14 for instructions on
making a table centrepiece.

TABLE CENTREPIECE
WITH LEAVES AND FLOWERS

*(Depicting Linnaea borealis, named after
Swedish botanist Carl von Linné, 1707–1778)*

MATERIAL:
linen, 10 threads per cm
(25 threads per in)

CUTTING SIZE:
60 × 60 cm (23½ × 23½ in)

FINISHED SIZE:
53 × 53 cm (21 × 21 in)

LACE:
2.25 m (88½ in)

THREAD:
DMC embroidery floss. Use 2
strands in the needle

After hemming, slipstitch the lace
in place all the way round the
centrepiece.

■	830	brown
•	732	dull green
◣	3345	darkest green
⊘	469	dark green
⊠	3347	medium green
Ⅼ	471	light green
‖	3687	dark rose
⊙	3326	medium rose
□	3689	light rose
⊟	732	dull green (backstitch)

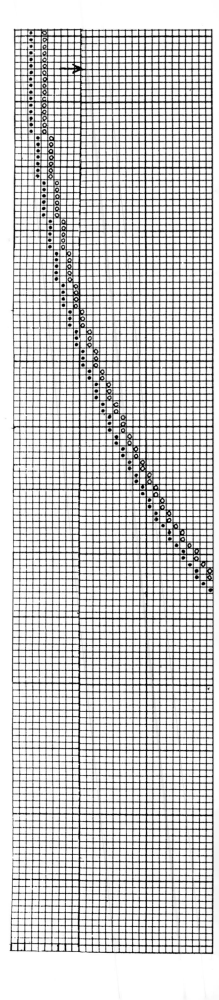

TABLE RUNNER WITH LEAVES AND FLOWERS

(Depicting Linnaea borealis, *named after Swedish botanist Carl von Linné, 1707–1778)*

MATERIAL:
linen, 10 threads per cm
(25 threads per in)
CUTTING SIZE:
72 × 30 cm (28½ × 11¾ in)
FINISHED SIZE:
66 × 25 cm (26 × 9¾ in)
THREAD:
DMC embroidery floss. Use 2
strands in the needle

See page 12 for instructions on
making a table runner.

▣	830	brown
●	732	dull green
◥	3345	darkest green
∕	469	dark green
✕	3347	medium green
Ⅼ	471	light green
Ⅲ	3687	dark rose
⊙	3326	medium rose
☐	3689	light rose
⊟	732	dull green (backstitch)

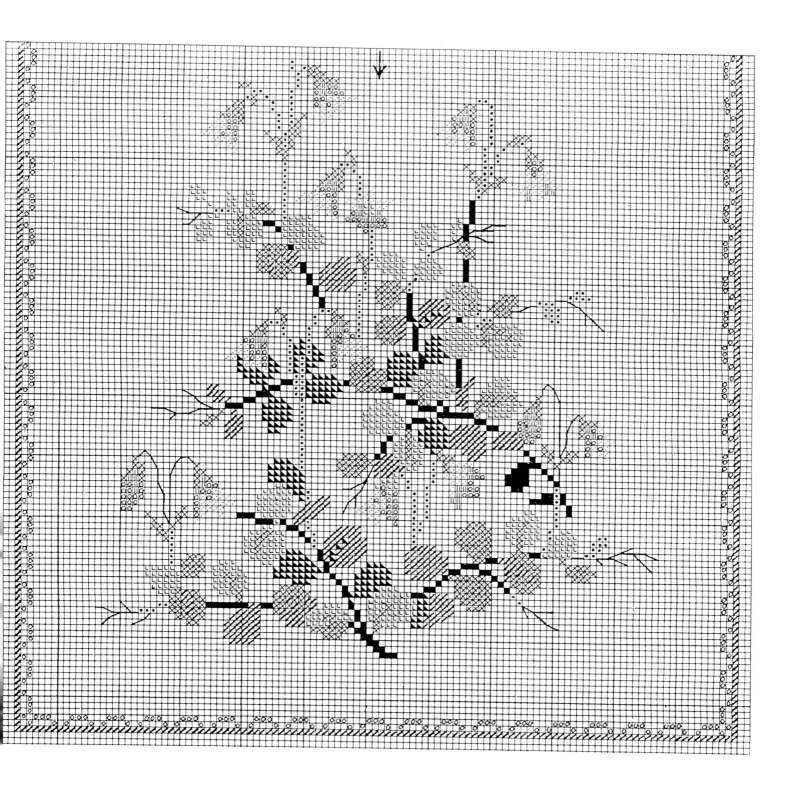

PICTURE WITH HAIRY GREENWEED

(Symbol of the province of Halland, Sweden)

MATERIAL:
linen, 10 threads per cm
(25 threads per in)

CUTTING SIZE:
28 × 35 cm (11 × 13¾ in)

FINISHED SIZE:
23.5 × 30.5 cm (9¼ × 12 in)

PIECE OF CARDBOARD:
21 × 28 cm (8¼ × 11 in)

THREAD:
DMC embroidery floss. Use 2
strands in the needle

◣	319	dark green
☒	469	medium green
⊡	471	light green
⬤	610	brown
⧄	731	dull green
◿	783	dark yellow
⊙	725	medium yellow
⊡	973	light yellow
▷	783	dark yellow (backstitch)

See page 11 for instructions on
making an unframed picture.

PICTURE WITH OAK LEAVES

(Symbol of the province of Blekinge, Sweden)

MATERIAL:
linen, 10 threads per cm
(25 threads per in)

CUTTING SIZE:
28 × 35 cm (11 × 13¾ in)

FINISHED SIZE:
23.5 × 30.5 cm (9¼ × 12 in)

PIECE OF CARDBOARD:
21 × 28 cm (8¼ × 11 in)

THREAD:
DMC embroidery floss. Use 2
strands in the needle

▣	869	brown
⊡	3011	dark dull green
◨	3012	medium dull green
☐	734	light dull green
◣	3345	darkest green
⧄	905	dark green
⊠	906	medium green
⊡	907	light green
⊟	869	brown (backstitch)

See page 11 for instructions on
making an unframed picture.

5
DESIGNS FROM
DENMARK

Denmark has probably the most mixed culture of the three Scandinavian countries. Owing to its geographical position, it has enjoyed direct connections and trade with other countries, and its artistic heritage has been influenced by the arts and crafts brought to it from other cultures. Many traders from neighbouring countries made their homes in Denmark, attracted by the easy-going nature of the indigenous people which made the country a pleasant place to live.

This national character is reflected in the heavy emphasis on flower subjects in Danish art. Here, the most famous porcelain design, 'Flora Dancia', originally commissioned by the Danish royal family for a dinner service to be presented to Tsarina Catherine II of Russia, has been

adapted to create a delightful framed cross stitch picture and tablemat. Another eighteenth-century porcelain design, 'Musselmalet', has been used to decorate a matching set comprising table runner, placemat and plate liner. Other floral designs have also been included, alongside native folk art and rustic styles.

This collection is completed by three designs taken from original paper cuts made by Danish fairy-storyteller, Hans Christian Andersen. These simple silhouettes are quick and easy to stitch using only one colour, so could be used on a variety of items to create a charming coordinated collection.

WALLHANGING WITH DANISH FOLK COSTUME

MATERIAL:
linen, 10 threads per cm
(25 threads per in)

CUTTING SIZE:
35 × 55 cm (13¾ × 21½ in)

FINISHED SIZE:
27 × 42 cm (10¾ × 16½ in)
approx

THREAD:
DMC embroidery floss. Use 2
strands in the needle

Make the hems on the long sides
8 threads deep. Measure 3 cm
(1¼ in) from top and bottom of
the embroidery and make the
casings for the fittings.

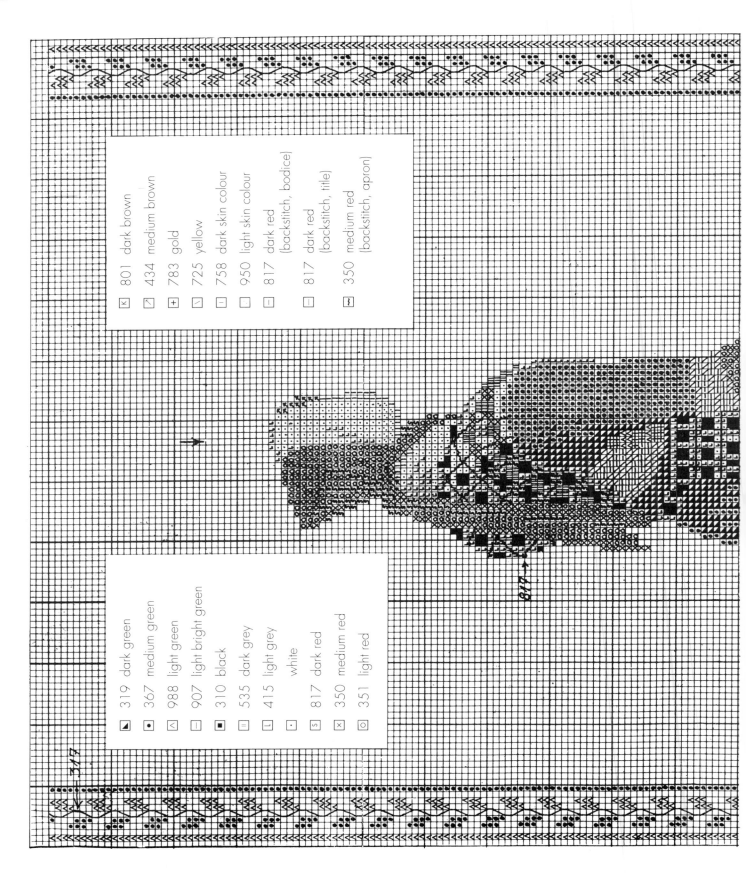

801 dark brown
434 medium brown
783 gold
725 yellow
758 dark skin colour
950 light skin colour
817 dark red (backstitch, bodice)
817 dark red (backstitch, title)
350 medium red (backstitch, apron)

319 dark green
367 medium green
988 light green
907 light bright green
310 black
535 dark grey
415 light grey
white
817 dark red
350 medium red
351 light red

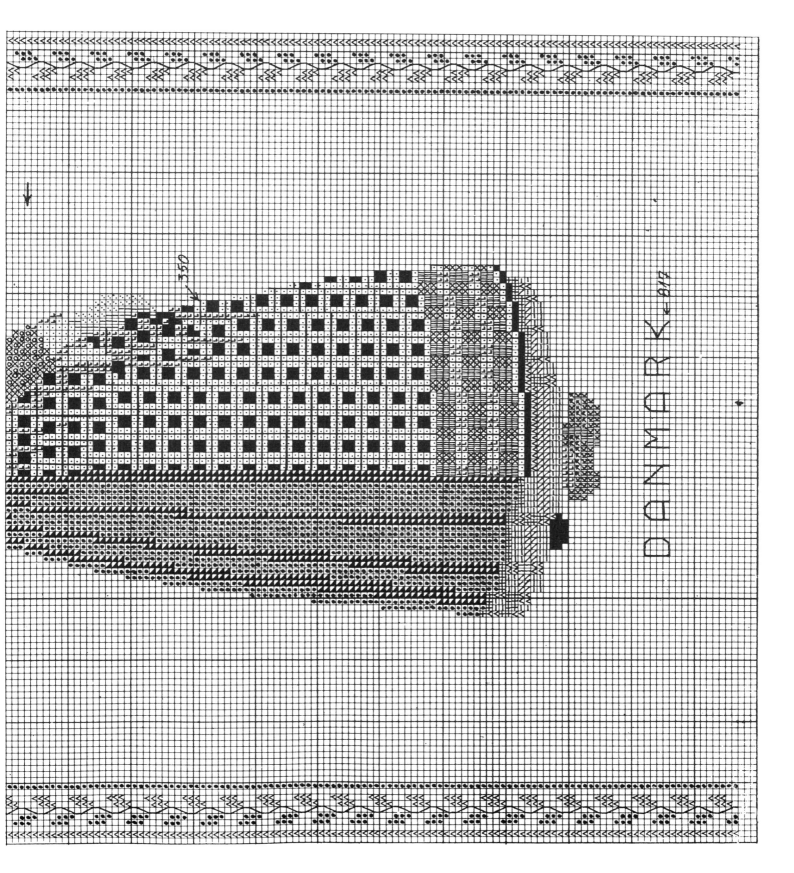

FRAMED PICTURE WITH 'FLORA DANICA' DESIGN

(Based on a design from the Flora Danica dinner service, original Royal Copenhagen, Denmark, about 1790)

MATERIAL:
linen, 10 threads per cm
(25 threads per in)
CUTTING SIZE:
35 × 28 cm (13¾ × 11 in)
FRAME (INSIDE):
29 × 21.5 cm (11½ × 8½ in)
THREAD:
DMC embroidery floss and fil d'or (gold metallic thread). Use 2 strands of floss and 1 strand of fil d'or in the needle

■	3345	darkest green
\	3346	dark green
✕	989	medium green
⊡	471	light green
⧄	733	dull green
◣	830	brown
⊡	832	gold
⊡	208	dark lilac
↗	209	medium lilac
⊟	211	light lilac
☐	307	yellow
L		fil d'or

Iron the finished embroidery and insert it in the frame.

PLACEMAT WITH 'FLORA DANICA' DESIGN

(Based on a design from the Flora Danica dinner service, original Royal Copenhagen, Denmark, about 1790)

MATERIAL:
linen, 10 threads per cm
(25 threads per in)

CUTTING SIZE:
52 × 43 cm (20½ × 17 in)

FINISHED SIZE:
46.5 × 38 cm (18¼ × 15 in)

THREAD:
DMC embroidery floss and fil d'or
(gold metallic thread). Use 2
strands of floss and 1 strand of
fil d'or in the needle

⊠	335	rose
■	3362	dark green
⧄	987	light green
•	832	gold
L		fil d'or
⊟	335	rose (backstitch)

See page 14 for instructions on
making rectangular table linen.

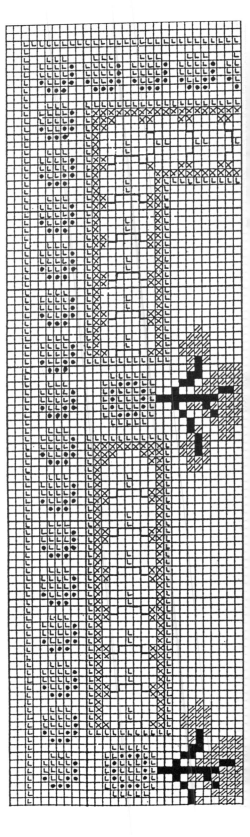

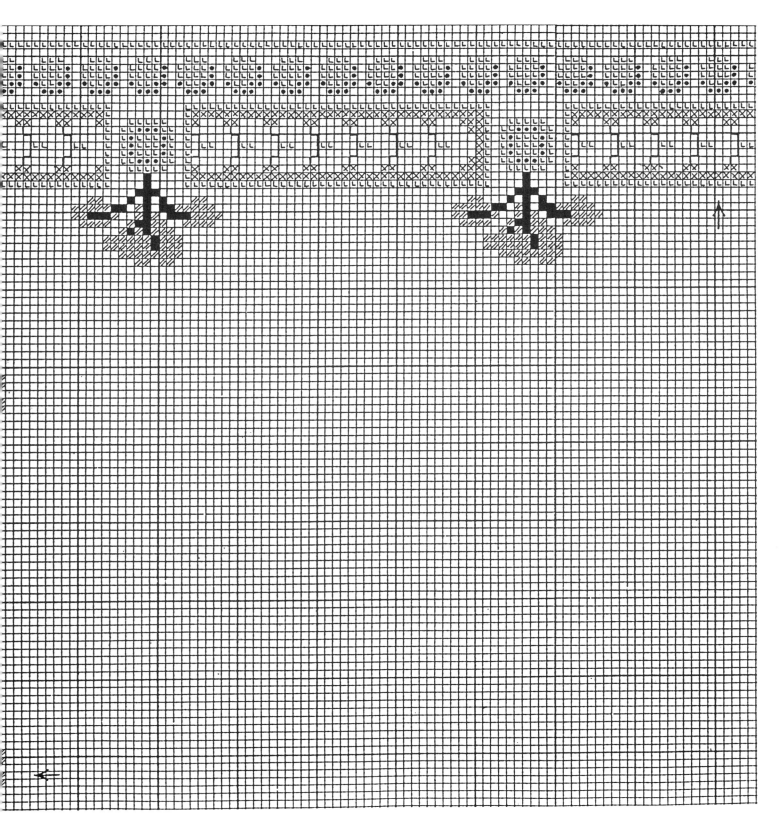

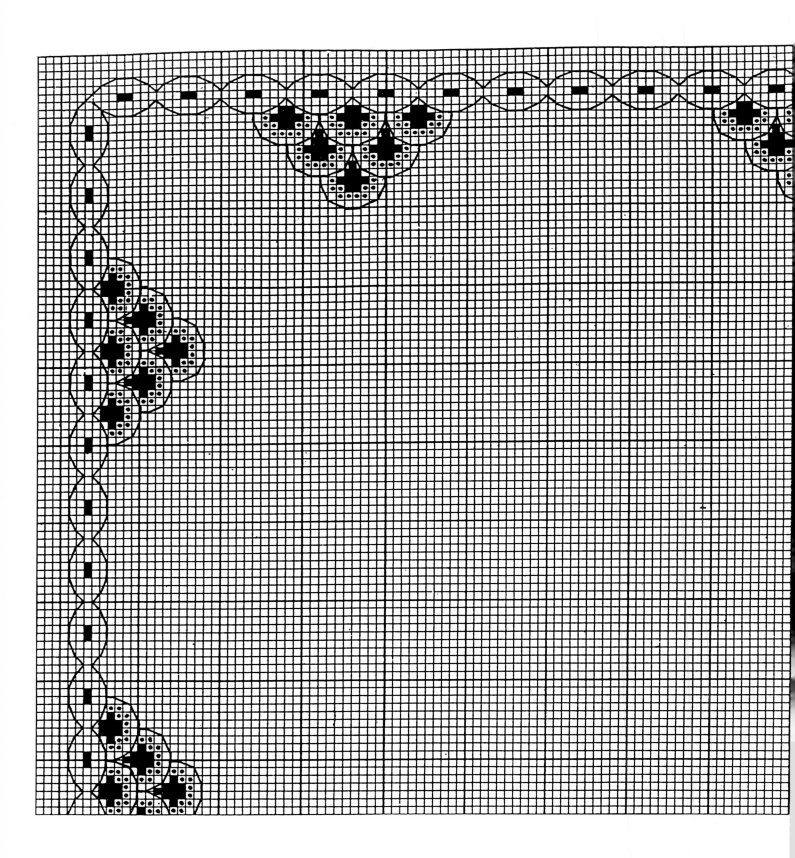

TABLE SET WITH 'MUSSELMALET' DESIGN

(Based on a porcelain design by Royal Copenhagen, Denmark, 18th century)

ORIGINAL COLOURWAY

- ■ 797 dark blue
- ⊡ 799 light blue
- ⊟ 799 light blue (backstitch)

RED COLOURWAY

- ■ 915 dark red
- ⊡ 602 light red
- ⊟ 602 light red (backstitch)

GOLD COLOURWAY

- ■ fil d'or for the whole design

MATERIAL:
linen, 10 threads per cm
(25 threads per in)

THREAD:
DMC embroidery floss and fil d'or
(gold metallic thread). Use 2
strands of floss and 1 of fil d'or
in the needle

See page 12 for instructions on making a table runner.

TABLE RUNNER
CUTTING SIZE:
75 × 42 cm (29¾ × 16½ in)
FINISHED SIZE:
70 × 37 cm (27½ × 14½ in)

PLACEMAT
CUTTING SIZE:
54 × 42 cm (21¼ × 16½ in)
FINISHED SIZE:
48 × 36 cm (19 × 14 in)

PLATE LINER
CUTTING SIZE:
20 × 20 cm (8 × 8 in)
FINISHED SIZE:
15 × 15 cm (5¾ × 5¾ in)

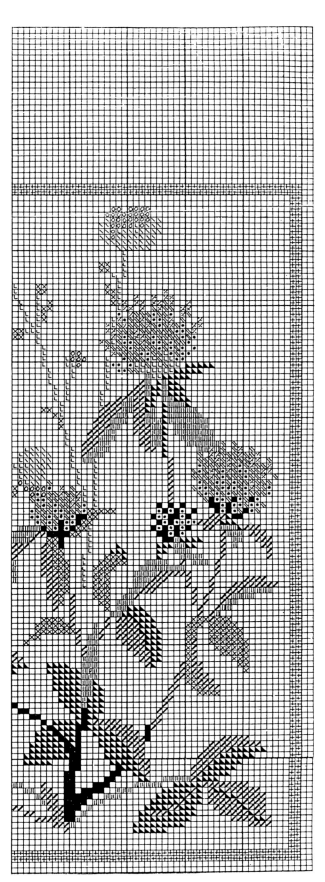

CUSHION
WITH WILD FLOWERS

MATERIAL:
linen, 10 threads per cm
(25 threads per in)
CUTTING SIZE:
42 × 45 cm (16½ × 18 in)
FINISHED SIZE:
34 × 38 cm (13½ × 15 in)
+ 2 cm (¾ in) edge
THREAD:
DMC embroidery floss. Use
2 strands in the needle

See page 13 for instructions
on making a cushion.

◣	3345	darkest green
⧄	904	dark green
⊠	905	medium green
L	471	light green
⫿	988	blue-green
⊡	3350	dark rose
◺	3688	medium rose
⧄	3689	light rose
⊙	444	yellow
◻	307	light yellow
◼	3011	brown
⊞	3023	beige
⊟	3023	beige (backstitch)
∼	988	blue-green (backstitch)

TRAYCLOTH
WITH FOLK ART DESIGN

MATERIAL:
linen, 8 threads per cm
(20 threads per in)

CUTTING SIZE:
52 × 44 cm (20½ × 17¼ in)

FINISHED SIZE:
47 × 39.5 cm (18½ × 15½ in)

THREAD:
DMC embroidery floss. Use 3
strands in the needle

◪ 806 dark blue
⊠ 597 light blue

See page 15 for instructions on
making a traycloth.

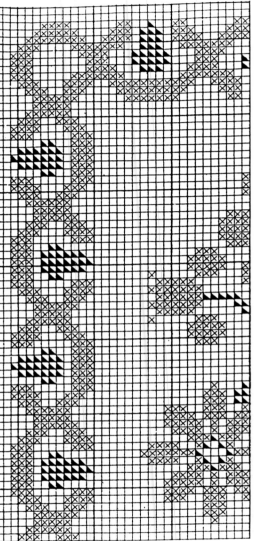

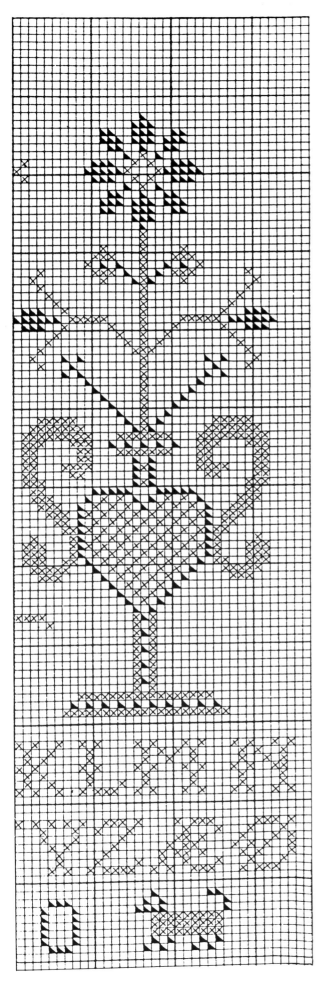

CUSHION IN DANISH RUSTIC STYLE

MATERIAL:
linen, 8 threads per cm
(20 threads per in)
CUTTING SIZE:
42 × 45 cm (16½ × 18 in)
FINISHED SIZE:
35.5 × 37.5 cm (14 × 14¾ in)
plus 1 cm (½ in) edge
THREAD:
DMC embroidery floss. Use 3
strands in the needle

⊠	321	red
◣	825	blue

See page 13 for instructions on making a cushion.

PLATE LINER WITH SILHOUETTED BALLERINAS

(Based on a paper cut by Danish fairy-storyteller Hans Christian Andersen)

MATERIAL:
linen, 10 threads per cm
(25 threads per in)
CUTTING SIZE:
22 × 22 cm (8¾ × 8¾ in)
FINISHED SIZE:
16.5 × 16.5 cm (6½ × 6½ in)
THREAD:
DMC embroidery floss. Use 2
strands in the needle

⊠ 796 blue

Finish with a hem 8 threads
deep.

PLATE LINER WITH
SILHOUETTED COUNTRY DANCERS

*(Based on a paper cut by Danish fairy-storyteller
Hans Christian Andersen)*

MATERIAL:
linen, 10 threads per cm
(25 threads per in)
CUTTING SIZE:
22 × 22 cm (8¾ × 8¾ in)
FINISHED SIZE:
16.5 × 16.5 cm (6½ × 6½ in)
THREAD:
DMC embroidery floss. Use 2
strands in the needle

☒ 796 blue

Finish with a hem 8 threads deep.

TOWEL AND CUSHION WITH SANDMAN MOTIF

(Based on a paper cut by Danish fairy-storyteller Hans Christian Andersen)

TOWEL

MATERIAL:
white Aida, 5½ stitches per cm
(13½ stitches per in)

CUTTING SIZE:
8 cm (3¼ in) × length required

FINISHED SIZE:
5 cm (2 in) deep

THREAD:
DMC embroidery floss. Use 2
strands in the needle

☒	3687	rose
⊟	797	blue (backstitch)

When finishing fold under the
long edges 2 stitches from the
embroidery.

CUSHION

MATERIAL:
piece of waste canvas 12 × 15
cm (4¾ × 5¾ in) approx, with 4
stitches per cm (10 stitches per in)

THREAD:
DMC embroidery floss.
Use 3 strands in the needle

☒	799	blue

See page 10 for instructions on
working with waste canvas.

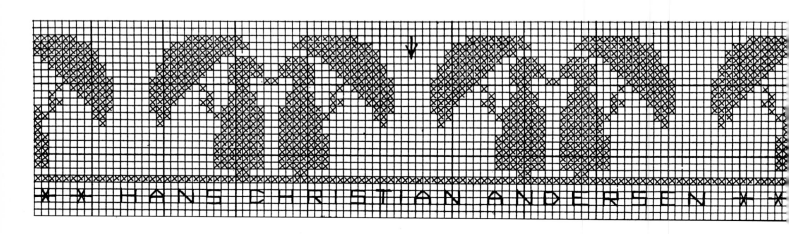

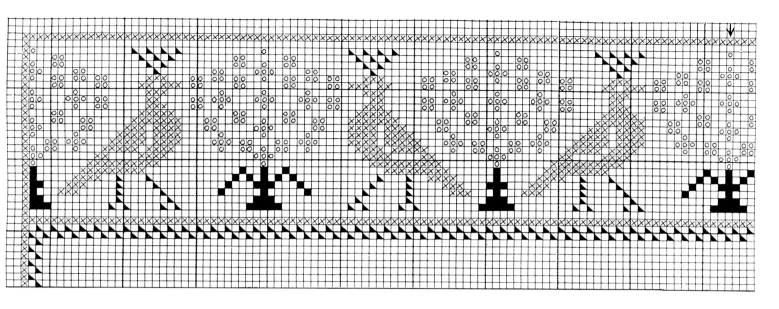

PLACEMAT WITH FOLK ART PEACOCKS

MATERIAL:
light beige Aida, 4½ stitches
per cm (11 stitches per in)

CUTTING SIZE:
40 × 50 cm (15¾ × 19½ in)

FINISHED SIZE:
45 × 35 cm (18 × 13¾ in)

THREAD:
DMC embroidery floss. Use 3
strands in the needle

■	731	brown
⊙	581	dull green
◤	806	blue
⊠	992	turquoise

See page 14 for instructions on
making rectangular table linen.

6

CHRISTMAS
CELEBRATIONS

Christmas is a festival that unites all Scandinavians, perhaps due to the long, dark winters experienced in these northerly climes. All three peoples love to celebrate Christmas, and even those who would not normally dream of taking up a needle and thread will delight in stitching an embroidery for the

festivities – many children no doubt worked their first stitches on a gift for family or friends at this time of year. Perhaps even the Viking women were busy with their sewing at Christmas time, making decorations for their celebration of the solstice on 21 December!

It is no coincidence that one of the finest stores in Denmark stages a permanent exhibition of Scandinavian Christmas decorations, which continues

 to enchant visitors from all round the world. The glittering collection of Christmas items in this chapter includes the best traditional Scandinavian designs, alongside some new and equally lively creations of my own. Through the use of brightly-coloured fabrics and metallic threads, combined

with traditional Christmas motifs such as hearts, bells and stars, I have put together a collection which I hope will inspire every embroiderer to pick up a needle and get stitching.

PLACEMAT WITH HEARTS

MATERIAL:
red Aida (imitation gauze), 5
stitches per cm (12½ stitches per in)

CUTTING SIZE:
50 × 40 cm (19½ × 15¾ in)

FINISHED SIZE:
46 × 36 cm (18 × 14 in)

THREAD:
DMC pearl cotton no. 5 and fil
d'argent (silver metallic thread).
Use 1 strand of pearl cotton and 2
strands of fil d'argent in the needle

☒	white pearl cotton
⊡	fil d'argent
⊟	fil d'argent (backstitch)

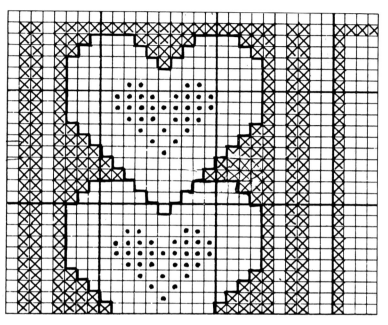

See page 14 for instructions on making rectangular table linen.

TABLE CENTREPIECE
WITH HEARTS AND ANGELS

MATERIAL:
red Aida, 4½ stitches per cm
(11 stitches per in)
CUTTING SIZE:
50 × 50 cm (19½ × 19½ in)
FINISHED SIZE:
44 × 44 cm (17¼ × 17¼ in)
THREAD:
pearl cotton no. 8

 white

See page 14 for instructions on
making a table centrepiece.

TABLE RUNNER
WITH HEARTS AND ANGELS

MATERIAL:
white Aida, 4½ stitches per cm
(11 stitches per in)
CUTTING SIZE:
62 × 35 cm (24½ × 13¾ in)
FINISHED SIZE:
57 × 30 cm (22½ × 11¾ in)
THREAD:
DMC embroidery floss. Use 3
strands in the needle

☒	666 red

See page 12 for instructions on
making a table runner.

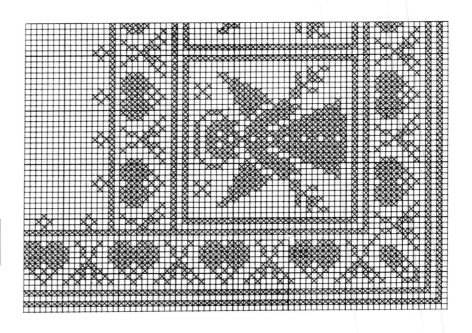

TABLE CENTREPIECE WITH
CHRISTMAS MOTIFS

MATERIAL:
white Aida, 4½ stitches per cm
(11 stitches per in)

CUTTING SIZE:
37 × 37 cm (14½ × 14½ in)

FINISHED SIZE:
31 × 31 cm (12¼ × 12¼ in)

LACE:
1.5 m (59 in) approx

THREAD:
DMC embroidery floss. Use 3
strands in the needle

⊠	350	red
◣	703	green
⊙	444	yellow

After hemming, slipstitch the lace
in place all the way round the
table centrepiece.

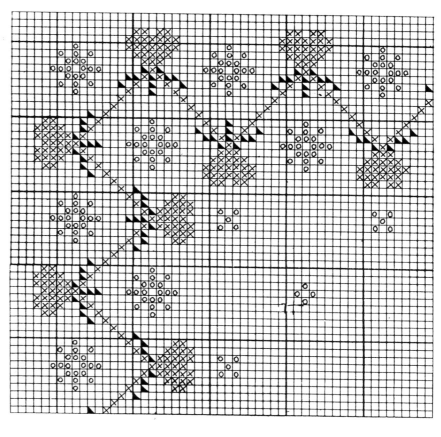

PLACEMAT AND NAPKIN RING
WITH GOLDEN STAR

MATERIAL:
white Aida, 4½ stitches per cm
(11 stitches per in)

PLACEMAT
CUTTING SIZE:
40 × 48 cm (15¾ × 19 in)
FINISHED SIZE:
36 × 48 cm (14 × 19 in)

NAPKIN RING
CUTTING SIZE:
11 × 15 cm (4¼ × 5¾ in)
FINISHED SIZE:
5 × 14 cm (2 × 5½ in)

THREAD:
DMC embroidery floss and fil d'or
(gold metallic thread). Use 1 strand
of fil d'or in the needle

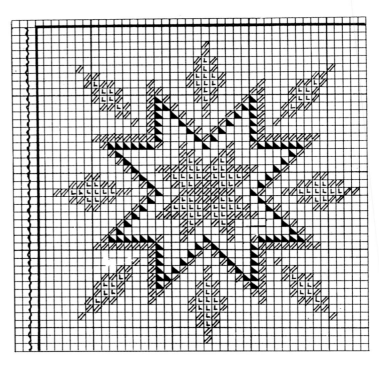

◤	783	gold
L	972	yellow
⫽		fil d'or
⁓	972	yellow (backstitch)
⊟	703	green (backstitch)

Instead of hemming the short
edges, carefully draw away
threads to create a 2 cm (¾ in)
fringe.

DOILIES WITH CHRISTMAS HEART

SQUARE DOILY

MATERIAL:
red Aida, 4½ stitches per cm
(11 stitches per in)

CUTTING SIZE:
15 × 15 cm (5¾ × 5¾ in)

FINISHED SIZE:
11 × 11 cm (4¼ × 4¼ in)

THREAD:
DMC embroidery floss and fil d'or
(gold metallic thread). Use 3 strands
of floss and 1 of fil d'or in the
needle

L	white
⊠	fil d'or
⊟	fil d'or (backstitch)

ROUND DOILY

MATERIAL:
blue Aida, 4½ stitches per cm
(11 stitches per in)

CUTTING SIZE:
12 × 12 cm (4¾ in)

FINISHED SIZE:
11.5 × 11.5 cm (4½ in)

BIAS TAPE:
white, 45 cm (18 in)

THREAD:
DMC embroidery floss. Use 3
strands in the needle

⊠	351	red
L		white

Once the excess fabric has been trimmed away, baste and then machine stitch the bias tape in place.

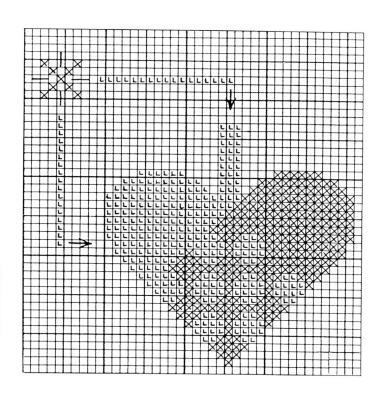

CHRISTMAS CANDLE

MATERIAL:
linen, 10 threads per cm
(25 threads per in)

DESIGN SIZE:
8 × 7 cm (3 × 2¾ in)

THREAD:
DMC embroidery floss. Use 2
strands in the needle

▣	831	brown
⊡	905	green
⊠	906	light green
⊞	608	red
⊟	972	yellow (backstitch)
⊟	310	black (wick)

This design could be used to
make Christmas greeting cards.

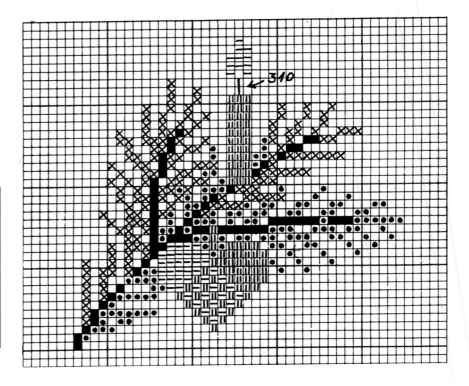

CHRISTMAS BORDER WITH BLUE STARS

MATERIAL:
white Aida, 4½ stitches per cm
(11 stitches per in)

CUTTING SIZE:
16 cm (6¼ in) deep × length
required

FINISHED SIZE:
7 cm (2¾ in)

THREAD:
DMC embroidery floss. Use 3
strands in the needle

⊡	798	dark blue
☒	809	light blue
Ⓛ	598	turquoise
☐	798	dark blue (backstitch)
⌇	809	light blue (backstitch)

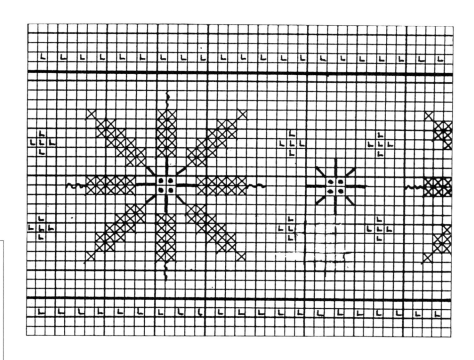

TABLE CENTREPIECE WITH HEARTS

MATERIAL:
white Aida, 4½ stitches per cm
(11 stitches per in)

CUTTING SIZE:
30 × 30 cm (11¾ × 11¾ in)

FINISHED SIZE:
25 × 25 cm (9¾ × 9¾ in)

BIAS TAPE:
rose, 90 cm (35½ in)

THREAD:
DMC embroidery floss. Use
2 strands in the needle

◣	600	dark red
▨	350	medium red
⊡	893	light red
☐	444	yellow

Once the excess fabric has been
trimmed away, baste and then
machine stitch the bias tape in
place.

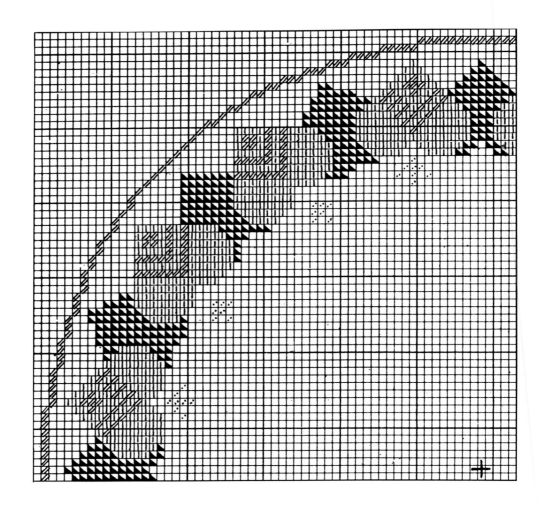

TABLE RUNNER AND TREE ORNAMENTS
WITH ANGELS

MATERIAL:
linen, 8 threads per cm
(20 threads per in)

TABLE RUNNER
CUTTING SIZE:
28 × 72 cm (11 × 28½ in)
FINISHED SIZE:
21.5 × 66.6 cm (8½ × 26¼ in)

TREE ORNAMENTS
CUTTING SIZE:
8 × 10 cm (3 × 4 in)
FINISHED SIZE:
5.5 × 7 cm (2¼ × 2¾ in)
CORD:
gold, 40 cm (15¾ in)

THREAD:
DMC embroidery floss and fil d'or
(gold metallic thread). Use 3
strands of floss and 1 strand of
fil d'or in the needle

▨	905	green
⊙	606	red
⊡	893	rose
◨	434	brown
△	553	lilac
◺	415	grey
☐	758	flesh
⊡	741	orange
⊠		fil d'or
⊟	905	green (backstitch, twigs)
⊟	434	brown (backstitch, sleeves)
⌁		fil d'or (backstitch)

Iron the finished embroidery and
glue it to a piece of cardboard.
Cover the edges on the back of
the cardboard with coloured
paper, preferably gold.

TABLE RUNNER AND HEART ORNAMENT
WITH PIXIES

MATERIAL:
white Aida, 4½ stitches per cm
(11 stitches per in)

TABLE RUNNER
CUTTING SIZE:
65 × 26 cm (25½ × 10¼ in)
FINISHED SIZE:
64 × 25 cm (25 × 9¾ in)
BIAS TAPE:
red, 180 cm (71 in)

HEART
CUTTING SIZE:
2 pieces, 31 × 27 cm
(12¼ × 10¾ in)
FINISHED SIZE:
29 × 26 cm (11½ × 10¼ in)
BIAS TAPE:
red, 95 cm (37½ in)

THREAD:
DMC embroidery floss. Use 3
strands in the needle

☒	606	red
⊟	3608	light lilac
⊡	352	dark rose
⊟	353	light rose
■	3371	darkest brown
∖	780	brown
Ⳑ	972	yellow
⊙	580	dull green
⌃	906	green
⧄	797	blue
⊟	3371	darkest brown (backstitch, wicks)
⊟	972	yellow (backstitch, rays)
⊟	606	red (backstitch, tassels)
⊟	780	brown (backstitch, eyebrows)

To complete the table runner and heart, once the excess fabric has been trimmed away, baste and then machine stitch the bias tape in place.

The heart ornament can be stiffened with iron-on interfacing.

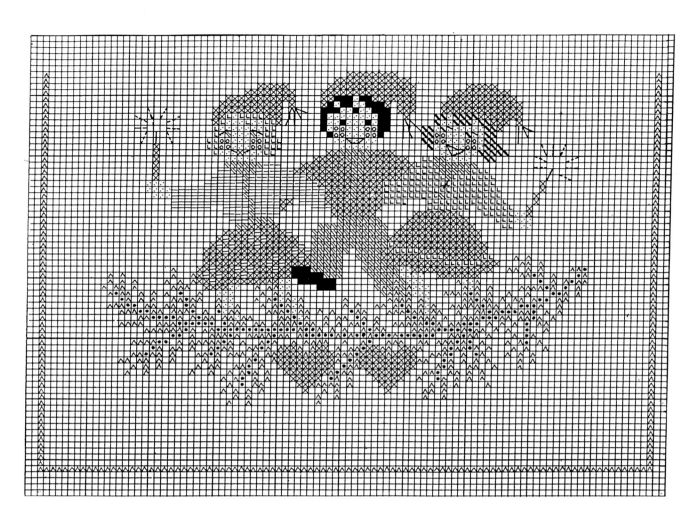

HEART-SHAPED TREE ORNAMENTS

MATERIAL:
white or red Aida (imitation gauze), 4½ stitches per cm (11 stitches per in)

CUTTING SIZE:
2 pieces, 8 × 8 cm (3 × 3 in) for each ornament

FINISHED SIZE:
6 × 5 cm (2½ × 2 in)

CORD:
red or gold, 35 cm (13¾ in)

THIN CARDBOARD:
2 pieces, 8 × 8 cm (3 × 3 in) for each ornament

THREAD:
DMC embroidery floss or fil d'or (gold metallic thread). Use 3 strands of floss and 1 strand of fil d'or in the needle

☒	742	yellow (white heart)
☒		fil d'or (red heart)

After ironing the finished embroidery, draw the outline of a heart on the material and embroider the stars. Cut out 2 heart-shaped pieces of cardboard and glue one each to the backs of the embroidery. Then glue the two pieces of cardboard together. When the glue has dried sew the card around the edge.

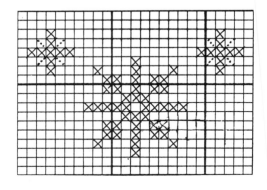

BELL-SHAPED TREE ORNAMENT

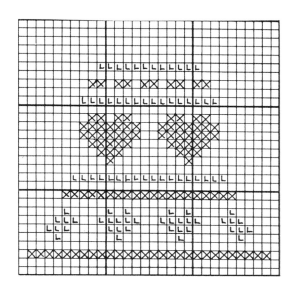

MATERIAL:
linen, 10 threads per cm
(25 threads per in)

CUTTING SIZE:
2 pieces, 7 × 7 cm (2¾ × 2¾ in)

FINISHED SIZE:
5 × 5.5 cm (2 × 2¼ in)

CORD:
gold, 20 cm (8 in)

THREAD:
DMC embroidery floss and fil d'or
(gold metallic thread). Use 2 strands
of floss and 1 strand of fil d'or in
the needle

⊠	606	red
L		fil d'or

Place the 2 embroidered bells
wrong sides together and
machine stitch together. Turn
inside out, and stitch the cord in
place around the long edges and
to form a hanging loop.

EGG COSY AND NAPKIN RING WITH HEARTS

MATERIAL:
linen, 10 threads per cm
(25 threads per in)

EGG COSY
CUTTING SIZE:
2 pieces, 12 × 12 cm
(4¾ × 4¾ in)

FINISHED SIZE:
8.5 × 9.5 cm (3¼ × 3½ in)

INTERFACING:
iron-on medium weight, 2 pieces,
12 × 12 cm (4¾ × 4¾ in)

RIBBON:
red, 25 cm (9¾ in)

NAPKIN RING
CUTTING SIZE:
9 × 15 cm (3¼ × 5¾ in)

FINISHED SIZE:
3.5 × 13.5 cm (1½ × 5¼ in)

THREAD:
DMC embroidery floss and fil d'or
(gold metallic thread). Use 2 strands
of floss and 1 of fil d'or in the
needle

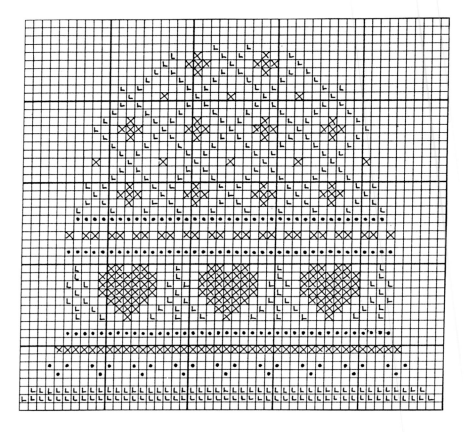

⊡	906	green
⊠	606	red
L		fil d'or

See page 15 for instructions
on making an egg cosy and a
napkin ring.